Umbrella Guide to
California Lighthouses

by
Sharlene & Ted Nelson

T.M.

UMBRELLA
BOOKS

An imprint of Epicenter Press

Editor: B.G. Olson
Cover design: Elizabeth Watson
Cover photo: Point Piños Lighthouse, Pacific Grove, photo by Ted Nelson
Pre-press production: Leslie Newman, Flora Wong, J. Stephen Lay.
Printer: McNaughton & Gunn

To order single copies of
UMBRELLA GUIDE TO CALIFORNIA LIGHTOUSES,
send $12.95 (Washington residents add 8.2% sales tax) plus $3.05 to:
Epicenter Press, 18821 64th Ave. N.E., Seattle, WA 98155.
Ask for our catalog. BOOKSELLERS: Retail discounts are available
from our trade distributor, Graphic Arts Center Publishing Co.,
Portland, OR, call 800-452-3032.

PRINTED IN THE UNITED STATES OF AMERICA
First printing, April, 1993

Foreword

S harlene and Ted Nelson wrote *Umbrella Guide to Washington Light houses* published in 1990. That concise history, with much new information, is a star among the numerous lighthouse books of recent years. Now the Nelsons have added another link to the world of lighthouse exploration with this fine effort on the lighthouses of California.

As with their first lighthouse book, their text is factual, concise, and interesting. The sections and chapters on the lighthouses and their keepers are enhanced with photos and maps showing how to reach the light stations. Visitor information is provided for the lighthouses that remain open.

The days of the manned light station have drawn to a close. Many stations live on adapted to new creative uses which allow them to be enjoyed by the public. In this book you will learn about two which are hostels, two that serve as inns, and several that are museums.

The *Umbrella Guide to California Lighthouses* is certainly a book you will want to read over and over again. And, one that you will want to keep in the glove compartment when a spare moment allows you to leave the beaten path and explore those narrow roads in search of the elusive lighthouse.

Wayne C. Wheeler, President
U. S. Lighthouse Society

iii

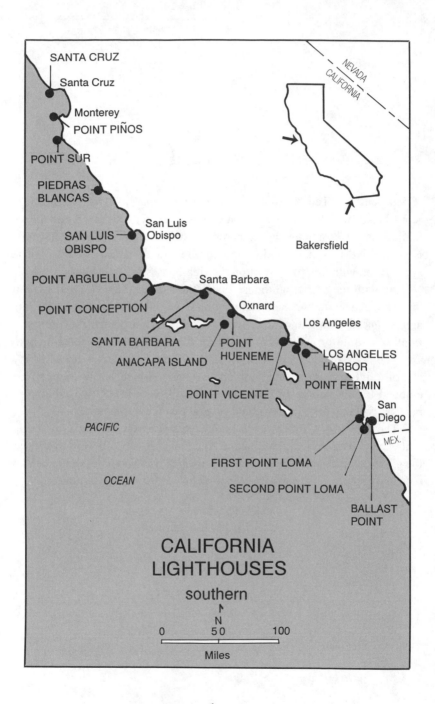

SANTA CRUZ

Santa Cruz

Monterey
POINT PIÑOS

POINT SUR

PIEDRAS
BLANCAS

San Luis
Obispo

SAN LUIS
OBISPO

Bakersfield

POINT ARGUELLO

Santa Barbara

POINT CONCEPTION

Oxnard

Los Angeles

SANTA BARBARA

POINT
HUENEME

ANACAPA ISLAND

LOS ANGELES
HARBOR

POINT FERMIN

POINT VICENTE

San
Diego

PACIFIC

MEX.

OCEAN

FIRST POINT LOMA

SECOND POINT LOMA

BALLAST
POINT

NEVADA
CALIFORNIA

CALIFORNIA
LIGHTHOUSES

southern

N

0   50   100

Miles

iv

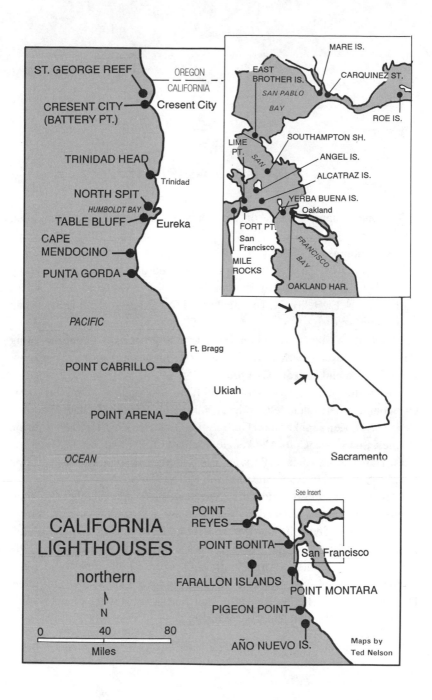

ST. GEORGE REEF

CRESENT CITY
(BATTERY PT.)

Cresent City

OREGON
CALIFORNIA

TRINIDAD HEAD

Trinidad

NORTH SPIT

HUMBOLDT BAY

TABLE BLUFF

Eureka

CAPE
MENDOCINO

PUNTA GORDA

PACIFIC

Ft. Bragg

POINT CABRILLO

Ukiah

POINT ARENA

OCEAN

Sacramento

See Insert

POINT
REYES

CALIFORNIA
LIGHTHOUSES

POINT BONITA

San Francisco

northern

N

FARALLON ISLANDS

POINT MONTARA

0   40   80

PIGEON POINT

Miles

AÑO NUEVO IS.

Maps by
Ted Nelson

MARE IS.

EAST
BROTHER IS.

CARQUINEZ ST.

SAN PABLO
BAY

ROE IS.

LIME
PT.

SOUTHAMPTON SH.

ANGEL IS.

SAN

ALCATRAZ IS.

YERBA BUENA IS.

Oakland

FORT PT.

San
Francisco

FRANCISCO
BAY

MILE
ROCKS

OAKLAND HAR.

Acknowledgments

We have many to thank for their support in writing this book begining with Wayne Wheeler, Tanya Rabbitt and Bill Morrison of the United States Lighthouse Society.

Personnel of the United States Coast Guard were helpful in many ways. They included Bryan Bender, Ian Brandy, Craig Bitler, Charles Curtian, Mark Englebrecht, Tom Jackson, J.C. Milberry, Deanna Sasse and Bruce Van Arsdale.

Special assistance was given by federal and state personnel including Beverly Ewoldscn, Marlene Greenway, Ron Jameson, Dewey Livingston, John Martini, and Howard Overton.

Museums, historical societies, and historians opened their files to us. Our contacts here included Craig Arnold, Bob Bolen, Michael Cropper, Gene Davis, Ken Franke, John Gail, James Gibbs, F. Ross Holland, Marion Holmes, Lila J. Lee, Colin Mackenzie, Richard McFarland, Diana McIntyre, Mark Hall-Patton, Richard Perkins, Frank Perry, Michael Redmon, Ralph Shanks, Sally West, Anne Stevens, and Bill Zerlang.

Lighthouse curators, docents, retired keepers and members of their families, and others interested in lighthouse history provided valuable help. They included Cliff and Ruthie Benton, Laverne Dornberger, Walter Fanning, Radford and Marie Franke, Bruce Handy, Mary Beth and Katie Harhen, Robert Lane, LeAnn Langford, Virgina Light, James and Betty Malone, Janise Nelson, William Olesen, Andrew Olund, Nancy Pierce, Dorothy Salles, Helga Settles, John and Barbara Sisto, Jerry and Nadine Tugel, Edward Wardell, and Ray Watson.

Table of Contents

SECTION 6   San Francisco Bay Beacons 97

SECTION 7   Lights to the Inland Waterways 127

SECTION 8   Redwood Coast Guardians 141

Introduction

California's shoreline meanders over 1200 miles from the sweep of southern beaches to the craggy headlands of the Redwood Coast. In 1542 the Portugese mariner Juan Rodriguez Cabrillo, under the Spanish flag, was the first European to explore the coast.

Spanish galleons laden with riches from Manilla sailed down the coast in the late sixteenth century. The English pirate Sir Francis Drake came to intercept them in 1579. Later, other explorers, fur traders, smugglers, hide traders, and whalers anchored in the coast's bays and inlets.

In 1848 gold was discovered in the Sierra Nevada foothills. Hundreds of vessels converged on San Francisco Bay, the gateway to the mines. The maritime trade spurred by the gold rush put more and more vessels at risk in the currents, fogs, and gales along California's coast. Congress authorized funds to begin building lighthouses in the new state.

A contract was let to the firm of Francis A. Gibbons and Francis X. Kelly to build the state's first seven lighthouses. In January 1853 the contractor's bark *Oriole* arrived in San Francisco from Baltimore with construction materials. By October 1853 the firm had completed the state's first lighthouse on Alcatraz Island. Eventually, over forty primary lighthouse stations and two lightship stations were established to guide mariners along California's coast, bays, and inland waterways.

Most of the lighthouses were built at remote locations. Generally, each station had dwellings for the light keepers and their families, cisterns or tanks to store water, storage sheds, other outbuildings, and perhaps a barn. Many had small wharfs where the lighthouse tenders tied when supplies were delivered and the inspector came. Most had a tower that raised the light to increase its range.

ix

The lens, the heart of most early California lighthouses was the Fresnel (Fray-NELL). This lens was perfected by the French optician, Augustin Fresnel, in 1822 but was not adopted for lighthouse use in the United States until 1852. It consisted of tiers of prisms above and below a central lens that combined to reflect and refract light into a powerful, horizontal beam.

The lenses came in different sizes called orders. The largest was a first-order lens standing over twelve feet high. The smallest, a sixth-order lens, was only sixteen inches high. The lenses, made in Europe, were shipped in sections, their brass frames numbered to guide reassembly.

The early source of light for the lenses was a lamp with carefully trimmed wicks. Thus, the term "wickie" was often applied to early light keepers. Over the years a succession of fuels was used including whale oil, rapeseed and lard oil, and finally, kerosene before the introduction of the electric light.

The lens and lamp were mounted in a glass enclosure called the lantern. The lantern protected the apparatus from the weather and formed the lantern room. A gallery surrounded the lantern to allow access for cleaning the glass panes.

The lenses could be configured in different ways to produce a characteristic that would distinguish one lighthouse from another. Stationary lenses, with an encircling central lens, produced a fixed light. Other lenses floated on mercury or rode on chariot wheels. The central lenses and prisms were arranged in panels, sometimes with colored screens. As the lens was rotated by a clockwork mechanism, and later by electric motors, a flashing light was produced.

Even the most powerful light was of little use in the fog. Many stations had fog signals, and some began with a fog signal and no light. Early keepers rang bells or fed coal or wood to steam-whistle boilers. Today, photoelectric cells activate electric horns.

The U.S. Lighthouse Service, under a Lighthouse Board, operated the lighthouses until 1910, when the Service was transferred to the Bureau of Lighthouses under the Commerce Department. The U.S. Coast Guard took responsibility for the lighthouses in 1939.

Automation has ended the era when the lights and fog signals required a keeper's care. Many of the original lenses are gone, replaced by aero beacons or small plastic lenses. Steel towers have replaced some early lighthouse towers, and the lightships have been replaced by buoys. Some lighthouse stations no longer exist.

Still much remains of the state's early lighthouse history. Many original lighthouses retain their historic character while still serving mariners. Many can be visited.

This is a guide to California's lighthouses, placed in the context of the state's history. The book describes the lighthouses, the supply vessels that serviced them, the lightships, and the men and women keepers who insured that the "light would not fail."

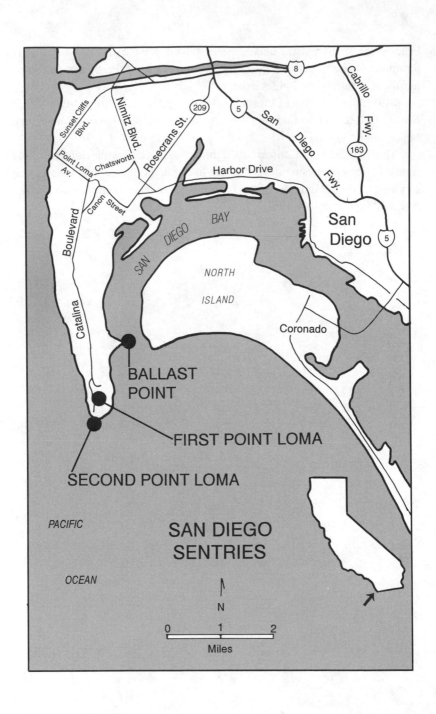

SAN DIEGO
SENTRIES

PACIFIC

OCEAN

N

0   1   2
Miles

Section 1

San Diego Sentries

Point Loma is a long, high hill forming a peninsula that extends south-ward into the Pacific near San Diego. Its gentle curve combines with a southerly flowing ocean current to create an eddy east of the point. Through geologic time the eddy has carried sediment from the Tijuana River to form North Island. A channel between the island and Point Loma leads to a natural harbor.

In September 1542 Juan Rodriguez Cabrillo, the first European to explore California's coast, sailed his two caravels, the *San Salvador* and the *Victoria*, beneath the point and into the bay. According to the journal of his voyage "...a heavy storm occurred, but since the port is good they did not feel it at all."

In 1779, Friar Junipero Serra established California's first European settlement near Old Town northeast of the point. The Spanish built a presidio on the hill above Old Town, a mission on the San Diego River, and a fort on the low point at the entrance to the bay.

Though out of the gold rush mainstream, San Diego Bay was a conve-nient harbor of refuge, and Point Loma was the southern most headland on the California coast. Thus, Point Loma received one of the new state's first lighthouses. Two others were later built on the peninsula; one near the site of the old Spanish fort, and a second Point Loma Lighthouse on a bluff below the original.

1

TED NELSON

Point Loma's first lighthouse in Cabrillo National Monument attracts thousands of visitors each year.

Chapter 1

Point Loma's First Lighthouse

Though officially decomissioned over a century ago, Point Loma's first light still shines. Every night a light beams from a stationary, third-order Fresnel lens toward San Diego. Every year a million visitors come to view the Pacific and see the lighthouse—a lighthouse built in the wrong place.

In 1851 the United States Coast Survey selected Point Loma, a 422-foot promontory, as a site for a lighthouse to guide ships sailing along the coast or into the harbor. The point was occasionally shrouded in fog, and one official questioned the site's suitability. Regardless, plans for the lighthouse moved ahead.

The schooner *Vaquero* arrived in 1854 with cement, lime, lumber, and workmen. It had been dispatched from San Francisco by the firm of Gibbons and Kelly. They held the contract to build California's first lighthouses. The men carved a road from Ballast Point up the steep hill to the lighthouse site. They quarried sandstone from Point Loma and salvaged tiles from the abandoned Spanish Fort Guijarros on Ballast Point.

The Cape Cod style dwelling with a tower rising through the center was finished in a few months, but the lantern and lens had not arrived. Here, as with other early west coast lighthouses, the towers had been designed to hold Argand lights and parabolic reflectors. During construction the Lighthouse Board decided to install the more efficient Fresnel lenses. When the lens finally arrived from France, the tower had to be reconstructed to accommodate it.

3

Finally, on November 15, 1855, James Keating, the first keeper, lit the light in the third-order Fresnel lens. Beaming from the tower 462 feet above the sea, Point Loma's light was the highest in the nation. F. Ross Holland in his book, *The Old Point Loma Lighthouse,* wrote that shortly after the light was exhibited one captain saw it thirty-nine miles at sea.

The lighthouse stood alone on the point. Far below, there was a whaling station at Ballast Point and a small trading center at La Playa where sailing vessels anchored. Inland, about seven miles, San Diego's adobes were clustered around a plaza, today's Old Town.

Turnover of keepers occurred frequently. During the lighthouse's thirty-six years, there were eleven principal keepers and twenty-two assistant keepers. Some stayed less than a year, possibly, because of living conditions. There were no separate quarters for assistant keepers until 1876 when two rooms were partitioned off in the woodshed.

Robert D. Israel was the exception. In 1871 Israel, forty-five and a long-time resident of San Diego, was assigned assistant keeper. Two years later he became the principal keeper, a position he held until the lighthouse was decommissioned in 1891.

Israel's wife, Maria, daughter of a prominent Spanish San Diego family, served as his assistant for three years. At night beneath the light's glow she appliqued quilts and stitched pillow shams. Maria was replaced in 1876, giving her more time for their sons, for gardening and gathering shells. She fashioned the shells into picture frames which now hang in the parlor of the restored lighthouse.

The boys often served as lookouts for the whalers and ships' pilots. Sighting whales or ships, they ran a tablecloth up the flag pole to signal the men in the harbor, red for ships, white for whales.

As predicted fog was a problem. High fog hid the lighthouse from mariners' view. Low fog hid all but a ship's masts from Israel's view. When Israel sighted them standing too close to shore, he fired warning shots from his shotgun. This was Point Loma's only fog signal.

Mariners' complaints about the fog brought change. In 1890 Ballast Point Lighthouse was built as a harbor light. In 1891 the present Point Loma Lighthouse near the beach below was lit to serve as a coast light. No longer needed, the old light was extinguished on March 23, 1891, and Israel and Maria moved to the new Point Loma Lighthouse.

By then the point had become a military reservation, and the boarded up lighthouse became army property. Sight-seers continued to follow a rutted road to the lighthouse. Some took souvenirs. Windows were broken. The outbuildings disappeared.

In 1913 a half acre where the lighthouse stood, became the Cabrillo National Monument. The plans were to remove the lighthouse and put in its place a 150-foot tall statue of explorer Juan Rodriquez Cabrillo. Funds were not forth coming, and the plans were dropped. In 1933 the Cabrillo National Monument was assigned to the National Park Service, and they restored the lighthouse.

During World War II, the point was closed to civilians. The lighthouse was painted a camouflage green, and used briefly by the Navy as a signal tower. In 1946 the lighthouse was returned to the Park Service, and a statue of Cabrillo was placed next to the lighthouse. For the lighthouse's one hundredth anniversary, the fourth-order Fresnel lens from Table Bluff Lighthouse was installed in the tower.

In 1957 the Cabrillo National Monument was the most visited monument in the U.S. including the Statue of Liberty. Over 953,000 people came to the cramped half-acre. It was soon enlarged to its current 144 acres. Later, the visitor center was built, and the Cabrillo statue was moved to its present site. Despite previous restoration, the lighthouse needed major repair. Beginning in 1980, the roof was replaced, the upper part of the old tower was torn down and a new one built.

Howard Overton, park historian, assisted in the work. His eyes sparkled when he described finding old Spanish tiles in the lighthouse walls. "I found a tile with the maker's thumbprint embedded in it," he said.

The Table Bluff lens was returned, and a third-order Fresnel lens from Mile Rocks Lighthouse was installed. Overton reassembled the lens in the tower and wired it for electricity. Though no longer used for navigation, the light turns on automatically at dusk and off at sunrise. A curtain on one side hides the light from ships at sea and protects the lens from the sun.

Furnishings in the lighthouse depict the Israel's lifestyle. The kitchen table is covered with a red, checkered tablecloth. An edge is rolled back, and playing cards are arranged on the table ready for a game of solitaire. Israel's grandson, Robert, said the keeper liked to play solitaire. After he used the same cards for three years, Maria, "…threatened to boil them up for soup."

Like early visitors, those today come to see the lighthouse, to watch migrating whales, and on a clear day to see the spectacular views of the Pacific and San Diego Bay.

Directions and Hours: Cabrillo National Monument is open daily, 9 A.M. to 5:15 P.M. with extended summer hours. Phone: (619) 557-5450.

U.S. LIGHTHOUSE SOCIETY

Ballast Point Lighthouse after Keeper Radford Franke planted his palm trees.

Chapter 2

Ballast Point Lighthouse

Ballast Point is a low, rocky spur jutting from Point Loma at the entrance to San Diego Bay. In 1796 the Spanish built a fort here to protect the bay. They called the point Punta Guijarros, Spanish for stones.

When Richard Henry Dana passed the point in 1835 aboard the brig *Pilgrim*, he wrote, "...the channel runs so near a low stony point that the ship's sides appeared to touch it." Dana's ship was bringing hides from Santa Barbara and Monterey to La Playa, a small settlement inside the point. The hides had been purchased with goods from New England. At La Playa they were cured, dried, and stored before shipment east. Outbound hide ships took on ballast from Punta Guijarros, and the point became known as Ballast Point.

The hide business declined in the 1850s, but shore whaling began to flourish. A whaling station, its pots bubbling with whale oil, existed on the point until 1886, four years before the lighthouse was established.

The Ballast Point Lighthouse, like the second Point Loma Lighthouse, was built to replace the original, fog-plagued Point Loma Lighthouse. One served as a harbor light, the other as a coast light. For nearly seventy years the Ballast Point light guided ships transiting San Diego Bay. Today, it is gone, and a submarine base occupies the point.

On August 1, 1890, the light was first exhibited from a fifth-order lens. It was mounted atop a thirty-five foot tower attached to one of the two Victorian dwellings. Near the water a fog bell hung in a small wooden house on stilts.

James R. Sweet was assigned to the point as an assistant keeper in 1903. Two years later he married Celia. She and James lived in one dwelling, and David Splaine lived in the other. "Old Captain Splaine was the lighthouse keeper at Ballast Point," said Celia. Splaine, an Irishman and Civil War veteran, had earlier served as assistant keeper at Farallon Islands, Point Conception, and the old Point Loma Lighthouse.

Celia described her husband's job as, "...tender of the buoys in the bay." Unlike most light stations, Ballast Point was a light attendant station. The keepers tended the tower's light as well as buoy lights that marked the channel in the ocean and bay. The keeper traveled in the station launch to each one. Often he had to chase off sea lions resting on the buoys before he cleaned the glass, fueled the light, or painted the buoy. When winds extinguished a light, the keeper steered the boat through high seas to re-light the lamp. In the early 1900s there were twelve buoys in the bay and several at the ocean entrance.

In 1914 Hermann Engel and his family left the cold winds of Point Bonita for warmer days at Ballast Point. The story of Engel's lighthouse days is told by his daughter, Norma Engel in *Three Beams of Light*. Mrs. Engel was paid twenty-five dollars a month to take care of the station while Engel and the assistant keeper tended the off-station aids. Each evening she stood the first watch from six to ten.

Though gray whales no longer frequented the bay as they did in the 1800s, one whale visited when Engel was tending the buoys. While Engel was coming home, the whale suddenly surfaced beneath the launch lifting it clear of the water, its prop spinning in the air. Then it slid from the whale into the water, the whale dove, and Engel, shaken but unharmed, continued home.

In 1928 a diaphone fog signal was installed, and the bell was retained as back-up. The diaphone's low, mournful sound caused irate neighbors to call and demand it be turned off.

A year before Engel retired in 1931, Radford Franke and his wife, Marie, arrived at the station. Franke, who was twenty-two years old, was then the youngest employee in the Lighthouse Service. He had served briefly on the San Francisco Lightship and then at Año Nuevo Lighthouse.

Though the Lighthouse Service was strict, days were enjoyable Franke said. Keepers were allowed two hours per week for shopping and six hours on Sunday to attend church. "You signed off the station and signed in when you returned," he said. "If you were an hour late, the time was taken off the keeper's annual vacation."

After the Coast Guard took over lighthouse management in 1939, Franke joined the Coast Guard. He became a Coxwain and continued to serve at Ballast Point.

During a wartime blackout when all navigation lights were turned off, Franke was glad the old fog bell was still hanging in the house on the beach. When a navy ship sailed too close to the point, Franke clanged the bell. The ship sailed safely by.

Franke's one irritant on the station were eucalyptus trees planted by an earlier keeper. Yet, it would be some time before he could make a change. Franke's youth prevented an early promotion, and older men were assigned to the station as principal keepers. In 1947 Franke became head keeper, and three years later he went to work to eliminate the eucalyptus.

Lobster fishermen anchored inside the point. Franke traded them left-over station paint for lobsters. Then he traded the lobsters to the gardener at the nearby naval station for twelve potted palms. After convincing Coast Guard inspectors that palm trees would improve the site's appearance, he proceeded with the planting.

Franke retired in 1957, and he and Marie now live in Point Loma. The station was razed in 1961. The lens went to storage at Cabrillo National Monument. Ken Franke, Director of the Maritime Museum of San Diego, and the Radford Franke's son, is working to secure the Ballast Point lantern and plans to display it with the lens at the museum.

The fog bell was sold to a scrap yard, then to a retired school teacher for five cents a pound. He hung it in his yard. Eventually it will be displayed at the museum.

Today, a minor light shines from Ballast Point where the submarine base stands. Until 1992 Keeper Franke's palm trees were the only vestige of the light station. Then they were removed to make room for an officers' club.

Directions and Hours: The museum, at 1306 North Harbor Drive, is open year round from 9 A.M. to 8 P.M. A new location is being considered. Phone: (619) 234-9153.

TED NELSON

Point Loma's second lighthouse can be seen from a road in Cabrillo National Monument.

Chapter 3

The Second Point Loma Lighthouse

Three lighthouses were established on the Point Loma peninsula. The second lighthouse called Point Loma has been in service for over a century, standing four hundred feet below its predecessor, below the high fog that caused the closure of the original lighthouse.

Scows delivered brick, mortar, and lumber to the new site in September 1889. The following spring two Victorian cottages, two cisterns, and a concrete foundation for the iron tower were completed. The tower arrived during the summer. Built for strength not aesthetics, its enclosed stairway and lantern were supported by four iron legs. It stood near the low bluff.

A new lens had been ordered from Henri La Paute of France. According to F. Ross Holland in *The Old Point Loma Lighthouse,* the handcrafted red and white prisms so pleased the maker that he asked for a delay in delivery to show the lens at a Paris show. It won a gold medal, and La Paute asked to exhibit it at a Chicago Exposition. Again the lens won a prize, and in the delay, the Lighthouse Service found another lens. Red panes of glass were installed to provide Point Loma's characteristic, and the prize winning lens was eventually installed at the Chicago Harbor Lighthouse.

San Diegans planned to celebrate the lighting of the new lighthouse. The *San Diego Weekly Union* reported that sailing parties and a moonlight picnic were planned, and the light would be lit, "...by a San Diego lady." The Lighthouse Board reported that, "On March 23 (1891) the light was exhibited for the first time..." through a third-order Fresnel lens. On this same day the old Point Loma light was extinguished.

11

Robert Israel, with his family, moved from the original lighthouse on the hill to serve as the first principal keeper. A year later, he resigned and was replaced by George P. Brennan, who had joined the Lighthouse Service in the 1880s and served at Point Arena before moving to Point Loma.

Brennan, his wife, Mary, and their six children arrived in San Diego aboard the steamer *Santa Rosa*. At an old wharf on the foot of 5th Street, they hired a carriage and rode to the lighthouse. "It was all new, and we were the second to live there," said Joe, one of the children. With them they brought some unforgettable days and high jinks.

The older children, Richard, George, and the twins, Joe and Nellie, rode to the Point Loma school house in a buggy pulled by their sway-back sorrel, Ping. In those days the route was, "...just a kind of cow trail." One of their school chums, Mary Eva Addis, recalled, "The Brennans came with bloody noses, and maybe only one would get there. They'd have awful fights. They were Irish you know...They had awful tempers, but I loved everyone of them."

One day the boys took Mary Eva and their sisters to the old lighthouse. They climbed up inside the tower and into the lantern room. Mary Eva stepped out on the gallery that encircled the lantern room, and the boys would not let her back in. "They scared me to death."

Mrs. Brennan died in 1895 while the family lived at the lighthouse. Keeper Brennan died in 1902. For a few months after his father's death, Joe tended the light until a new keeper arrived.

In 1912 Captain W.A. Beaman was principal keeper and Malcom Cady was assistant keeper. Operating supplies for the lighthouse were delivered by a Lighthouse Service tender, but the keepers bought their necessities in town. On shopping day the Cady family hiked up the hill and down the other side to Fort Rosecrans where they caught a boat to San Diego.

A fog-signal was installed in 1913. Maritime traffic was increasing rapidly matching the growth of San Diego and neighboring communties. The signal would, "...enable vessels to enter San Diego Bay during fogs which occasionally prevail during the winter and spring months." The building for the air sirens was built in front of the tower. The fog signal required a keeper, and a third dwelling was added to the station.

About the same time, the red screens were removed from the lens, so the light characteristic became flashing white. A few years later city water was piped to the point.

In the 1920s radio beacons were installed at several lighthouses including Point Loma. At the time radio beacons were "state of the art" in assisting ships navigating in fog. Electric wires were strung to the lighthouse to operate the radio beacon, and the kerosene burning incandenscent oil vapor lamp in the lens was replaced by an electric light. Even though the lighthouse was wired for electricity in 1926, the keepers waited for seven more years before they could exchange their kerosene lamps for electric light bulbs.

When the Coast Guard assumed management of the nation's lighthouses in 1939, Milford Johnson was assistant keeper at Point Loma. He was assigned to the station in 1931. Like some Lighthouse Service keepers, Johnson chose to join the Coast Guard and continued to serve at the light station. He retired as head keeper in 1951.

The station is now automated. The original Fresnel lens, a radio beacon, and two-tone diaphone fog signal are maintained by Coast Guard personnel from Aids to Navigation San Diego. The original dwellings are occupied by Coast Guard officers and their families. Though the station is off-limits, you can see the lighthouse from a road that winds down to the shore in the Cabrillo National Monument. The paved road long ago replaced the "cow trail" used by Ping with her buggy full of Keeper Brennan's children.

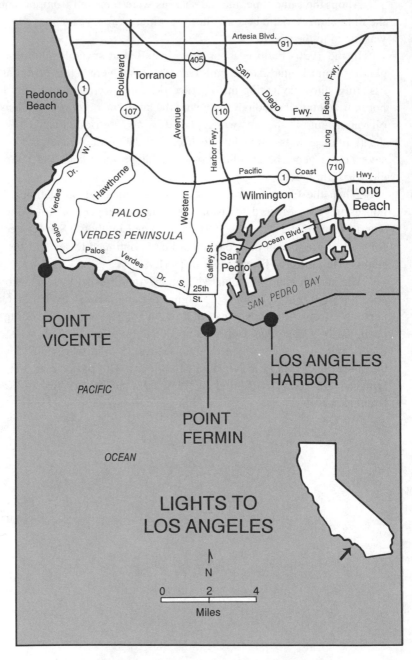

Section 2

Lights to Los Angeles

The southern California coastline sweeps northwest from San Diego until it is interrupted by the Palos Verdes Peninsula that juts south. The peninsula, with its high hills and bluffs, forms the west end of San Pedro Bay.

In October 1542 Juan Rodriguez Cabrillo became the first European to anchor beneath the Palos Verdes hills. He named the bay, Bahia de Los Fumos or Bay of Smokes, for the many fires set by the peninsula's Indians. From there Cabrillo sailed north. In 1602 Sebastian Vizcaino renamed the bay, Bahia de San Pedro, even though he was instructed by the Spanish government not to change names given by Cabrillo.

In the 1830s, San Pedro Bay became the port serving the Pueblo de Los Angeles, then the largest settlement in California. The port and pueblo were connected by nearly thirty miles of dusty road. Hides and tallow were brought to the bay by ox-cart and lightered to waiting vessels in exchange for silks, jewels, satins, and housewares.

The port continued to grow, but not until 1874 was the area's first lighthouse established at Point Fermin. Later, the Los Angeles Harbor Lighthouse was built at the end of the port's western breakwater, and the Point Vicente Lighthouse was built at the southwestern point of the peninsula.

TED NELSON

Point Fermin Lighthouse with its restored lantern stands on the grounds of a Los Angeles City Park.

Chapter 4

Point Fermin Lighthouse

Near the Point Fermin Lighthouse a viewpoint overlooks Los Angeles-Long Beach Harbor. Cranes and tank farms dot Terminal Island. Container ships and cruise liners come and go. While watching this scene, it is hard to visualize how the harbor looked in 1874 when the Point Fermin light first shone.

Five years before the lighthouse was built, southern California's first railroad had been completed between Los Angeles and Wilmington on inner San Pedro Bay. A low sandbar, later the backbone of Terminal Island, lay across from Wilmington, connected to Deadman's Island in the outer bay by a breakwater. A shallow channel led to the rail terminus. Larger vessels, unable to sail the channel, anchored outside and lightered their cargo ashore at Wilmington or San Pedro.

After the railroad began operating, local businessmen and mariners appealed to the Lighthouse Service for a lighthouse on Point Fermin. A similar request had been made in 1854 by Phineas Banning when he began to develop the harbor.

By 1872 a lighthouse site had been selected on Point Fermin. The point was a bold cliff on the bay's western edge rising one hundred feet above the water. Another year passed while the Lighthouse Service obtained title to the land.

Wagon loads of redwood and fir, delivered by ship, were hauled to the sage-covered bluff in early 1874, and by late fall the Victorian lighthouse was completed. A once planned fog signal was never built.

17

Weeks later the first keepers, Mary L. Smith, and her sister, Ella, moved into the new lighthouse. Both were experienced light keepers, who had tended the Ediz Hook light in Washington Territory before coming to Point Fermin. On December 15, 1874, they lit the lamp and wound the apparatus that rotated the fourth-order Fresnel lens. Red screens produced a red and white flashing characteristic.

Two years later, their nephew, Norman R. Smith, came to visit. Norman, who was eighteen and lived in the mid-west, was traveling before beginning college. He caught a steamer in San Francisco and sailed for San Pedro. In a newspaper feature he wrote, "We landed there in a lighter after Captain Johnson had signalled the lighthouse as we passed it that I was on board." Norman noted that, "The lighthouse was just under the old adobe fort on the bluff and opposite Deadman's Island."

On May 8, 1882, Mary wrote in the station log, "Mr. George N. Shaw and wife arrive at the station with a portion of their effects and are occupied in getting the remainder from Wilmington..." This entry marked the end of Mary's and Ella's years with the Lighthouse Service

Captain Shaw, a Civil War veteran and former sea captain, was fifty when he and his wife moved to Point Fermin. He had served briefly at Point Reyes and Yerba Buena Island. Shaw's entries in the log were routine, "...boxing shade trees...Sabbath...tending lantern...," added to daily weather reports. His last entry, November 7, 1904, read, "Former Keeper retires this day, George N. Shaw. Irby H. Engels, took charge of this station at noon today."

While Engels was keeper, there were rumors that Point Fermin would be torn down. Construction was underway on the Los Angeles Harbor Lighthouse, and there was talk of a new lighthouse on Point Vicente which would render Point Fermin's lighthouse obsolete. The light was still operating when Engels resigned in 1917.

The next keeper, Willie Austin, and his family filled the lighthouse with six children. One more, Paul Fermin Austin, was born after they arrived. Austin tended the light for eight years, then tragedy struck.

Mrs. Austin died after an operation, and Austin died two months later. "My father just seem to waste away," said Thelma, their oldest daughter. "In fact he died of a broken heart, since they had been together all these years in the lighthouse work."

Thelma and her sister, Juanita, decided to continue tending the Point Fermin light, because, "…we had a sacred duty to perform: to promulgate the heroic work which our parents started." Gradually, family members moved away, and Thelma stayed on in the empty house tending the light until 1927.

That year the Los Angeles City Recreation and Parks Department contracted with the Lighthouse Service. The Department assumed operation and care of the lighthouse in exchange for the land and use of the lighthouse as a residence for the superintendent. By then the light had been electrified and could be operated by the turn of a switch.

On the morning of December 9, 1941, Mr. and Mrs. Oscar Johnson turned the tower's light off for the last time. With the advent of World War II the navy took over, removed the lens, dismantled the lantern room, and built a box-shaped lookout atop the tower. Local residents called it the "chicken coop." After the war, a steel tower with an automatic light was established at the edge of the bluff to replace the original light.

Even though park personnel lived in the old lighthouse, the Coast Guard in the late 1960s considered tearing it down. This spurred two long-time San Pedro residents, William Olesen and John Olguin, into action.

Both remembered the lighthouse from boyhood days. "I first saw the light in 1912, when I came down the coast on my father's lumber schooner," said Olesen. He was then eight years old.

Olguin visited the lighthouse with his father and two brothers in 1923. "I had my picture taken as a boy with the lighthouse keeper's daughter (Thelma)," he said.

Olesen, a retired boat builder, and Olguin, retired director of the Cabrillo Beach Marine Museum, set to work to refurbish the lighthouse. They gathered local support and moved their way through the bureaucracy. In 1973 the lighthouse was entered on the National Register of Historic Places.

A short time later, the Coast Guard found the original lighthouse blueprints. Olesen started to work. He tore the "chicken coop" off, and using the original plans, started building a new lantern room. Olesen and Olquin, with help from off-duty firemen, finished the new lantern room just days before the lighthouse's centennial celebration.

Thelma Austin Cunningham and the Oscar Johnsons cut an 1100-pound birthday cake as they stood near the tower that again looked as it did when Norman came to visit Mary and Ella.

Directions and Hours: The lighthouse is closed to the public but can be seen at the park. Follow Gaffey Street west through San Pedro.

Chapter 5

Los Angeles Harbor Lighthouse

The Los Angeles Harbor Lighthouse marks the end of the two-mile long San Pedro breakwater and guides ships into Los Angeles Harbor. Often referred to as the "Angel's Gate" light, it was commissioned in 1913. Standing on a large concrete block at the east end of the rock breakwater, the lighthouse also marked the outcome of a long battle over the location of southern California's major seaport—a battle of railroads and politics, not ships.

In 1874, the year that the Point Fermin Lighthouse was established, the Southern Pacific Railroad Company acquired the railroad that connected Los Angeles with Wilmington. Though there was still no transcontinental rail service to Southern California, the small port at Wilmington on inner San Pedro Bay was begining to grow.

In 1875 a rival railroad was completed from Los Angeles to Santa Monica. A wharf was built, and the new port began to take business away from San Pedro Bay.

A year later the Southern Pacific's transcontinental line reached Los Angeles. To protect its position at San Pedro Bay the Southern Pacific bought then closed the rival line to Santa Monica. The Los Angeles to Wilmington line was extended to the town of San Pedro.

With these moves the backers of a major port on San Pedro Bay felt their position was secure. Planning began for a breakwater to protect larger vessels anchored in the outer San Pedro Bay.

But, the battle over the seaport's location had just begun. The Santa Fe Railroad reached southern California, built a branch line to Redondo Beach,

21

Los Angeles Harbor Lighthouse has survived earthquakes and a scrape with a battleship.

and commenced a port operation there. Then Collis P. Huntington became President of the Southern Pacific Railroad. He favored Santa Monica as the major port. He reestablished its rail service and reopened its port in 1893.

Between 1891 and 1897 three commissions were appointed by Congress. They investigated the best location for a deep water port from Santa Monica to Capistrano. Each one reported in favor of San Pedro. Each time Huntington used his influence to block action. The *New York World* commented, "…is this a government by the people, for the people, or a government by Mr. Huntington, for Mr. Huntington?" Despite Huntington's efforts, Congress authorized funds for a breakwater on San Pedro Bay.

Work began in 1889 and was completed in 1910. The breakwater extended into San Pedro Bay from the east side of Point Fermin. Three years later the lighthouse was completed. It was built around twelve steel columns. The octagonal first story was sheathed with steel plates. The ten-sided, second story and cylindrical top three stories were covered with cement. The steel columns were covered with black pilasters that contrasted with the white of the building. The resulting Romanesque appearance was unlike any other west coast lighthouse.

The station's first light was exhibited, March 1, 1913, from a fourth-order Fresnel lens. Its light source was an oil incandescent vapor lamp. The light flashed white every fifteen seconds. It also had two compressed air sirens powered by gas engines.

Three keepers tended the station. The quarters were too small to include families, and they lived in town. A few months after the station began operation, second assistant keeper Hughes was suspended for assaulting principal keeper, John Olsen. No reason was given for the assualt, but Olsen added in the suspension report, "All keepers at this station are instructed that in the future no distilled or malt liquors are to be brought to this station."

Fuel for the lamp and fog signal and other station supplies were delivered by tender and lightered to the breakwater. When keepers wanted to leave the breakwater, they traveled in the station launch. Using a derrick, they lifted the launch from its cradle and lowered it into the water.

Even though the lighthouse was a short distance from town, storms often isolated the keepers. One storm lasted for several days. Waves thirty-five feet high crashed against the lighthouse. According to local lore, the keepers claimed that the wave battering from this storm caused the lighthouse to tilt.

The sturdy tower was tested again during an earthquake on March 10, 1933. The first assistant keeper reported that at 5:54 p.m., "Earth shock of great intensity shook tower violently for a period of 20 seconds, approximately. Lens, light, radio beacon, and tower O.K. Considerable mercury shaken out of lens base. Tower swaying east and west." Long Beach was hard hit. One hundred fifteen lives were lost and hundreds were injured.

Years later the lighthouse again missed being knocked off its foundation. One night a keeper was thrown from his bed after a shattering blow to the concrete platform. Gaining his senses, the keeper raced to the window and saw the running lights of a battleship. The ship, only scratched by the scraping, sailed on. The incident was reported, but for years remained in navy files labeled, "confidential."

As the communities bordering the harbor grew, lights from homes and

businesses created "light noise," and mariners had a difficult time distinguishing the light from background lights. Thus, in the early 1930s a green,
translucent cover was placed over the lens. This created a green flashing
light, the only one in a major California lighthouse.

The Coast Guard assumed lighthouse management in 1939, and coast
guardsmen tended the light until it was automated in 1973.

Storms in the early 1980s battered the lighthouse, breached the breakwater, and severed the electric cable to the lighthouse. Rather than repair
the cable that might be cut again by the sharp, rip rap rocks, diesel
generators were fired up to power the light, fog signal, and the radio
beacon.

Three years later, the Coast Guard decided to install solar generated
batteries at the lighthouse. Solar power was cheaper than diesel. It was
being used successfully at lighthouses on the east coast and on buoys and
small harbor lights on the west coast.

This was a heralded event. Los Angeles Harbor would be the first
lighthouse on the west coast to rely on solar power. The original Fresnel
lens weighing 300 pounds was removed, and a thirty-pound plastic lens
replaced it. The fog signal's range was shortened, and the light's visibility
was reduced from twenty-two miles to fifteen.

Boat owners soon began to object. "It looks like a light in San Pedro,"
said one. Another said he use to see the original light from Catalina Island,
but couldn't see the new one.

The Coast Guard experimented with boosting the power, then decided
that the busy harbor needed a light of higher intensity. In 1989 a new lens,
similar to the original, was placed in the tower, and the generators were
fired up again. Today a green light, the hallmark of the Los Angeles Harbor
Lighthouse, still flashes in the tower.

The original Fresnel lens is on display at the Los Angeles Maritime
Museum in San Pedro. Near the city's waterfront you can see the pictur-
esque lighthouse from Cabrillo Beach or a viewpoint on Gaffey Street.

Directions and Hours: Los Angeles Maritime Museum is at berth 84 at
the foot of 6th Street in San Pedro. Open Tuesday through Sunday from 10
A.M to 5 P.M. Closed Christmas, Thanksgiving and New Years. Phone
(310) 548-7618.

Chapter 6

Point Vicente Lighthouse

Point Vicente is a high, steep sided point on the southwestern end of the Palos Verdes Peninsula. The Lighthouse Commissioner's report of 1914 describes the point as, "...the most prominent of the California shoreline between Point Loma and Point Conception, a distance of 220 nautical miles." Despite its prominence, the point's lighthouse was one of the last to be built on the west coast.

The point's Spanish name belies its English origin. This point and Point Fermin to the east were named by Captain George Vancouver. The names honor Spanish mission friars who assisted the English explorer on his voyage down the California coast in 1793. A spelling error by Vancouver, or a later editor of his journals, caused the name to be spelled Vincente until the error was corrected after the point's lighthouse was built.

In 1914 many reasons were given by the Lighthouse Commissioner to support a request for funds for a lighthouse and fog signal on Point Vicente. The point was said to obscure the Point Fermin light, "...from steamers approaching on the usual courses from northward until within 4 miles of Point Vincente." It was also noted that, "Freight and passenger traffic is very heavy along this part of the coast and will be materially increased with the opening of the Panama Canal."

After Congress approved funding for the lighthouse in 1916, progress was slow. Elaborately financed real estate schemes were underway on the Palos Verdes Peninsula, causing the Lighthouse Service difficulty in acquiring the lighthouse station property. Condemnation was threatened, then postponed, and in 1921 the site was finally acquired.

In the meantime, construction costs had risen causing further delays, but in 1925 the three keepers' dwellings, the outbuildings, and the fog-signal building were completed. The fog signal could be heard a distance of three miles.

In the spring of 1926 the station's electrical generating plant finally illuminated the point's light, a five-hundred-watt lamp within a third-order Fresnel lens. The lens was mounted on a fifty-five foot white, cylindrical tower made of reinforced concrete. The tower's height combined with the point's prominence placed the lens' focal plane 185 feet above the water. The white light flashed twice each twenty seconds.

Other kinds of beacons were added at the point in 1934, and later the Coast Guard constructed several buildings and tall radio antennas near the lighthouse. The radio station and radio navigation beacon were operated until 1980 when the equipment became outdated.

During World War II, a smaller lamp was installed and blackout curtains were at the ready. After the war, a larger lamp was reinstalled. When Rancho Palos Verdes residents complained about the regular flashes of light on their bedroom walls, the landward side of the lantern was painted white. As the lens revolved behind the painted lantern, a gossamer like shadow appeared, giving rise to ghost stories that persist today.

The point's light was automated in 1971, and the original Fresnel lens still flashes white each twenty seconds. On weekends and holidays, the old radio station, with new equipment, crackles to life. Tuned to marine channels, members of the Long Beach Coast Guard Auxiliary stay in contact with aircraft piloted by auxiliary members. Distress calls are monitored, the boat's location pinpointed by direction finder, and assistance is dispatched from the Coast Guard at Long Beach.

Coast Guard personnel, serving elsewhere, are quartered in the station's buildings, and the lighthouse grounds are closed to the public. However, near the lighthouse is the Point Vicente Interpretive Center with an attractive park. The park and center, operated by the City of Rancho Palos Verdes, afford good views of the lighthouse tower and Santa Catalina Island across San Pedro Channel. Whale watching is popular during the months of December through April. Exhibits at the center tell the cultural and natural history of the peninsula.

Directions and Hours: The park and center are reached by Hawthorn Boulevard and Palos Verdes Drive south or west. Hours are 10 A.M. to 5 P.M. in the winter and 10 A.M. to 7 P.M. in the summer. Phone: (310) 377-5370.

TED NELSON

Point Vicente Lighthouse can be seen from a nearby park.

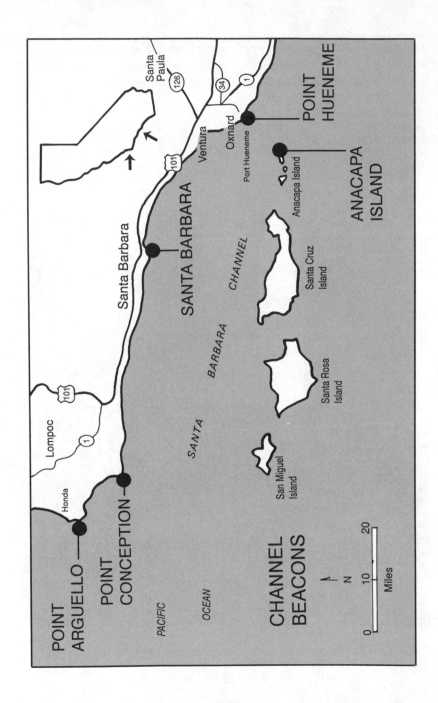

Section 3

Santa Barbara Channel Beacons

The Santa Barbara Channel extends sixty-three miles from Point Hueneme to Point Conception. Between these points the coast trends in a near westerly direction. The channel is bounded on the south by four islands, San Miguel, Santa Rosa, Santa Cruz, and Anacapa.

Explorer Juan Rodriguez Cabrillo sailed the channel in October and November of 1542. After sailing farther up the coast, Cabrillo returned to San Miguel Island where he died of an injury suffered in a fall on its rocky shore.

Early mariners noted a sheen on the channel's water and the odor of tar. The natural seepage of hydrocarbons was the precursor of the offshore oil drilling rigs that dot the channel today.

The channel is treacherous, plagued by strong currents and often thick fogs. Winter storms bring strong southeasterly winds, and in the fall severe north-easterlies blow from the desert. These conditions in combination with the jagged islands have caused the loss of over one hundred large ships and many more small vessels.

Four lighthouses were built along the channel at Santa Barbara, Point Conception, Point Hueneme and Anacapa Island, and though north of the channel, Point Arguello's lighthouse is included in this section. It became forever linked with the channel's history when seven U.S. Navy destroyers drove ashore near there in 1923. Their commander thought his ships had cleared the channel entrance at Point Conception.

This first lighthouse at Point Hueneme was removed when Port Hueneme was built.

Chapter 7

Point Hueneme Lighthouse

Point Hueneme Lighthouse stands at the end of Oxnard's tree-lined streets. The concrete tower is barely visible behind the fence of a naval installation. A Port Hueneme dock extends outside the fence.

Nothing remains of the original 1874 Victorian lighthouse, and development obscures the once great stretches of sand that formed this remote point. The dredged Port Hueneme channel has swallowed a small slough that lay behind the sand dune where the first lighthouse stood for sixty-six years.

Point Hueneme is at the southeast end of the Santa Barbara Channel. From the mariners view it had little to distinguish it and was considered a navigational hazard.

In 1872 the Lighthouse Service proposed building a first class, fog signal at Point Hueneme. They changed plans, and two years later built a lighthouse in a design similar to the Point Fermin Lighthouse. Its light from a fourth order Fresnel lens atop a fifty-two foot tower was first exhibited the same day as Point Fermin's, December 15, 1874.

A month earlier, Samuel Ensign had arrived from Pigeon Point. To prepare the new station he, "...went to San Buenaventura (Ventura) to purchase necessary supplies," and helped the Lighthouse Service lampist set-up the lamp and lens.

Two days before the light was exhibited assistant keeper Melvin Giles, his wife, and two sons arrived from San Francisco aboard the steamer *Constatine*. All went well for a couple months, until one morning Ensign

31

found Giles asleep while on watch. He was reprimanded. It happened again. This time Ensign discovered the lamp still lit, and "...No curtains up and sun shone brightly." Even so, eight months after arriving at Point Hueneme, Giles was promoted to principal keeper at Pigeon Point.

Later, Ensign with assistant keeper Korts, kept the light and lens in good order, but neglected the grounds and buildings. In August 1878 Korts was fired, and so was Ensign for "...physical incapacity to discharge the duties of Station Keeper."

Though serious, the dismissals were not as tragic as events that occurred three years later. Log entries by J. Apairthon McFarland, and in his absence by assistant keeper, John Ross, were routine daily weather and watch reports. "Easterly wind-strong, breeze-clear warm. Mrs. Ross 1st watch, Capt. Ross 2nd watch."

The day after Christmas 1881 the log read, "Assistant Keepers wife (Sarah Ross) was confined of still born twins this morning at 8 a.m." Sarah died in January, and shortly after, McFarland and Ross left Point Hueneme.

Blowing sand had been a problem since the lighthouse's beginning, and in 1876 a ten-foot high, board fence was built around it. Still, the sand sifted in, and the keeper planted a variety of seeds in 1880. He found lupine and burr clover worked best.

For fourteen years the tower's light flashed white. In 1889 it was changed to fixed red, then changed again in 1892 to occulting white. In 1899 a new lens was installed showing a white, flashing characteristic. This lens now rotates in the present lighthouse. Though years late, a fog signal had been installed by the early 1920s.

Possibly, the keeper who served longest at Point Hueneme was Walter White. During his twenty-one years there, he and his family witnessed major changes at the point. White, his wife, Frances, and three children, Laverne, LeRoy, and Beatrice moved from Point Montara to Point Hueneme in 1927.

Mrs. Laverne White Dornberger, a resident of Vashon Island, Washington, remembered her years at Point Hueneme. She was six years old when they arrived.

Nearby were sand dunes and beach cottages. At high tide the lighthouse was surrounded by water. The Whites lived downstairs, while Laverne's bedroom was upstairs next to the assistant keeper's quarters. His livingroom, kitchen, bathroom, and bedroom, were accessed by outside stairs.

There were no "modern" conveniences. A hand-pump at the sink pumped rain water from the cistern. Kerosene lamps served as household light. The lens was rotated by a clockwork mechanism. In the watch room, there was a worn Bible issued years earlier by the Lighthouse Service.

Laverne, like her brother and sister, had her chores. "It was my job to clean the brass," she said. Daily she polished the brass dust pan and kerosene lamp bases, and washed the lamp chimneys.

When her father was "...laid up for several months with rheumatism," Laverne and her mother, a small woman, took over his duties. To start the lens rotating, it required the strength of both to wind the clockworks. The chains hung down inside the tower and into the assistant keeper's bathroom. "We'd wind and wind," said Laverne.

During prohibition mainland beaches along the Santa Barbara Channel were favored drop places for smugglers. One day Laverne and a friend were walking the beach near the lighthouse. Scattered along the sand, they found wicker wrapped bottles filled with rum. They dug a hole in the sand, buried the bottles, and hurried home to tell Keeper White. When they returned, the tide had washed all traces away.

When electricity was installed around 1933, brass lamp polishing ceased. Still, the Whites kept the station to Lighthouse Service standards. When the Inspector arrived, it was a "white-glove inspection," said Laverne. He checked the top of the refrigerator for dust and even looked inside.

The efforts paid off. White was awarded the superintendent's "efficiency star" for three years beginning in 1937. The first time for the Point Hueneme Lighthouse.

Changes began soon after. Two new dwellings were built, the light was extinguished and a temporary light displayed—all to clear the way for the dredging and construction of Port Hueneme.

"A yacht club bought the lighthouse," said Laverne, and it was barged across the harbor. "It sat there negelected and was finally torn down."

The present lighthouse is a Moderne style, cement structure with a fifty-two foot tower rising from a fog-signal building. The 1899 lens from the old lighthouse was installed when the new tower was completed in 1941.

Though the new lighthouse was under Coast Guard management,

White was close to retirement and decided to remain a civilian. He retired from Point Hueneme in 1948.

Coast guardsmen tended the light just as the early lightkeepers did, turning it on at dusk and off at sunrise. They, also, conducted tours until the light and fog signal were automated. Today, the light rotates twenty-four hours and is inspected weekly and serviced monthly by personnel from Coast Guard Station Channel Islands Harbor.

Because the lighthouse is inside a guarded naval installation, it is off limits to visitors.

U.S. COAST GUARD

The Santa Barbara Lighthouse was destroyed by an earthquake in 1925.

Chapter 8

Santa Barbara Lighthouse

The Santa Barbara light, a twenty-four foot, white tower, stands on a high mesa west of the city's harbor. Grass grows at its base. Coast Guard buildings separate it from the road. All that remains of the original lighthouse, tended by one woman for forty years, is the name.

Early in 1856, contractor George Nagle and his family arrived from San Francisco. They set up camp on the lonely, chapparal-covered mesa where they lived while Nagle built the lighthouse. By summer Albert J. Williams, his pregnant wife, Julia, and their daughter moved into the Cape Cod style lighthouse.

Williams and Julia were both from Maine. Their second daughter was born at the lighthouse in October. On December 1, 1856, Williams lit the lamp in the fixed, fourth-order Fresnel lens. It originally showed red, but a few years later was changed to white.

After four years, Williams became restless with the confinement. He left and bought a small farm nearby. When his replacement left, the Lighthouse Service asked Williams to return. He refused, but Julia agreed, and she was appointed keeper on February 13, 1865.

Julia, a short, slender woman, was forty-one. Since there was no fog signal, she could tend the station alone, and still raise their five children. Her keeper's routine began just before sunset when she lit the lamp. At midnight she trimmed the wick and checked the lamp's fuel. Rising early, she extinguished the lamp, covered the lens with a cloth, and started baking. By the time everyone gathered for breakfast, hot loaves of bread were on the table.

Two or three times a year the Lighthouse Service delivered lamp fuel, wicks, cleaning rags, and aprons. The aprons were man-size. Julia cut them down to her size. Repairs, like replacing a fence blown down in a gale, were done by Lighthouse Service crews.

In 1900 Julia's seventeen-year-old grandson, True Maxfield, came to live at the lighthouse to work for Frank, Julia's son. Frank leased and farmed the lighthouse property. True told about his five years at the lighthouse in a 1963 interview with F. Ross Holland.

When True arrived, Julia was seventy-six. "She was very energetic and always very well and strong," said True. "...and she always kept it (the light) in perfect condition." At night she slept on a low sofa in the parlor. It was close to the circular wood stairs leading to the tower.

On week days visitors came to see the lighthouse and Julia, and on Sundays True hitched the horses to the carriage and drove Julia to church in Santa Barbara. Other than Sunday outings Julia seldom left the station. Frank did her shopping and brought her vegetables from the farm.

In 1905 Julia fell off the sofa, and broke her hip. Thinking it was only a bad bump, she continued her work. A few days later she was hospitalized. She was eighty-one. The fall ended Julia's light keeper's career. She died in 1911.

Julia was succeeded by Mrs. Jones, then Mrs. Caroline Morse in 1910. Three years later, M.A. Weeks and his family moved to the lighthouse.

In the early 1920s the Lighthouse Service recommended building a new lighthouse closer to the mesa's edge. Then nature changed the plans.

Early on June 29, 1925, an earthquake shook Santa Barbara. Acting keeper Weeks, son of the late keeper, was sleeping in a nearby building. Rushing outside, he saw half the lighthouse destroyed. The tower lay in pieces on the ground. Scrambling through the wreckage, Weeks rescued his mother, sister, brother, and visiting relatives. They suffered only bruises.

Four days later, a light shown from a temporary, frame tower. Construction of a new lighthouse was considered. Instead, the present, automated tower with a minor optic was built in 1935. It serves mariners as did the original, one of the west coast's first sixteen lighthouses.

Chapter 9

Point Conception Lighthouse

Two features stand out on a map of California. One is the 130 degree angle made by the political boundary between California and Nevada, its apex in Lake Tahoe. The other is the nearly ninety-degree turn taken by the coastline at the north end of the Santa Barbara Channel, its apex at Point Conception.

This point was selected by the Lighthouse Service to receive one of California's first seven lighthouses under the contract with the firm of Gibbons and Kelly. Often called the "Cape Horn of the Pacific," the point was known to mariners for its heavy northwest gales and, "...a marked change of climatic and meterological conditions,...off the point, the transition often being remarkably sudden and well defined."

Construction of the lighthouse was delayed when the contractor's vessel, the *Oriole* was sunk delivering construction supplies to Cape Disappointment in Washington Territory. Still, by the summer of 1854, the dwelling and tower were complete, awaiting inspection by Lighthouse Inspector Major Hartman Bache.

Bache climbed up the 220-foot high bluff to the site and found the work to be shoddy. He ordered more work done, but in 1855 the *Santa Barbara Gazette* complained that construction was still so, "...insecure and unworkmanlike that on different occassions (the lighthouse) has been damaged by the weather." Also, like several of the first lighthouses, the tower was too small to accommodate the first-order Fresnel lens to be delivered from France. The brick tower rising through the center of the one and one-half story, Cape Cod style keeper's dwelling had to be torn down and rebuilt.

TED NELSON

Point Conception's original first-order Fresnel lens is still used in the point's second lighthouse.

Keeper George Parkinson arrived in 1855, before the lens was delivered. Historian Jerry MacMullen stated that Parkinson found the lighthouse full of Indians whom he had to shoo away. Parkinson also found that his new station was sixty-five miles from Santa Barbara, "...the nearest point at which supplies can be obtained (and) the road is only passable at low water..." The nearest wood was six miles away and the nearest water six hundred yards away. On top of all that he was not receiving his pay.

Parkinson directed the assembly of the revolving first-order Fresnel lens and the lamp apparatus. It was landed through the surf from the schooner *General Pierce* in September, 1855. The white flashing light was finally shown for the first time on February 1, 1856. Keeper Parkinson resigned exactly six months later.

In 1872 the fog bell was replaced by a steam whistle, and soon after another keeper's cottage was added.

Weather and frequent earthquakes continued to take their toll on the lighthouse. In 1875 the Lighthouse Board proposed to tear down the Cape Cod's rooms, leave its tower standing, and build new cottages to house the four keepers.

Nothing was done about the request, and in 1880 the Lighthouse Board changed its plans and its tactics. The Board told Congress that the old building was now "insecure" and, "...wooden supports (are) placed against the tower to hold it up." The Board stated that a new tower and dwelling should be built on a lower point on the bluff, and without immediate appropriations this, "...most important...light must be discontinued."

Congress responded, and on June 20, 1882, the station's original lens shone from a new tower. This lighthouse would have satisfied even Major Bache. The plastered brick walls were sixteen to twenty-four inches thick. They had a skirt of granite. Attached to the fifty-two foot high tower was a spacious workroom with a large fireplace, and a large oil storage room.

The new lighthouse stood on a bluff below the point where the old tower had stood. Its focal plane was 133 feet above the sea. Construction materials had been lightered ashore from a ship anchored in Coho Bay, east of the point. They were hauled by cart and wagon to the point and lined or slid down to the bluff below.

Until after the turn of the century, the keepers and their families lived in a collection of dwellings that failed to match the lighthouse's grandeur. Except for a new cottage built in 1882, their homes included a made-over oil house and the Cape Cod dwelling, its tower gone and its sides held together with iron rods.

In 1906, a two-story frame dwelling was built at the top of the steps leading down to the lighthouse. It housed two keepers and their families with six rooms and a bath for each. In 1912, a new keepers dwelling finally replaced Parkinson's home on the point.

A 1946 *Saturday Evening Post* article featured keepers Max Schlederer and Charley Hellwig. They had, "...no electric lights, no telephone, no communications with...neighbors." On his watch, Max did, "... nothing but sit there and watch that light." Max pointed out that even a tiny piece of carbon could plug the vaporizer of the kerosene burning lamp, causing it to cool and then to flare up in flame.

Two years later, a 1,000-watt electric, mercury vapor light replaced the old kerosene lamp. On February 15, 1973, the station was fully automated. For a time it was monitored from Point Arguello, fifteen miles to the north. By then, most of the older dwellings had been removed. Newer ones, now abandoned, stood in their place.

The light is now tended by personnel from Coast Guard Station Channel Islands Harbor. Coast guardsmen, Bruce Van Arsdale and Tom Jackson made a recent trip.

From Lompoc they passed the Jamala Beach road and drove through rolling hills to a gate secured by seven padlocks. A wild pig darted across the road as they passed a sandy moor. Cattle gazed at the official vehicle. They parked near a shop where the main keepers' dwelling once stood.

Descending the steep steps to the bluff below, they unlocked the lighthouse's massive doors. Inside, the wood paneled watch room was empty as was the oil room with its circular bins that once held barrels of lard oil and then kerosene.

They climbed the circular, iron stairs beneath the soft glow of prisms imbedded in the lantern room floor. Their voices echoed as they passed the clockwork mechanism that once turned the lens. At the len's base, they noted the need for new chariot wheels, still in stock at Oxnard. In the lantern room, they found the ten-foot high, sixteen-panel Fresnel lens, still turning regulary as it has for 136 years.

With all in order they returned to their base. Bruce and Tom appreciated their opportunity to tend the light that still marks the "Cape Horn of the Pacific."

The lighthouse is closed to the public.

Chapter 10

Point Arguello Lighthouse

A mariner once said, "Sailing a boat into the (Santa Barbara) channel between San Miguel Island and Points Arguello and Conception is like sailing into the eye of a needle." Ships passed Point Arguello as they sailed south to Point Conception where they made the turn into the channel. Fog frequently obscured Point Arguello, a long, narrow point projecting from a rounding in the coastline. Off shore rocks increased the hazards. Some ships failed to make it pass the point.

Navigation aids here, a light on a steel tower, a foghorn, and radio beacon, all automated, still serve mariners. The point's original lighthouse is gone. Flowers planted by keepers' wives grow wild. On the open uplands, stand empty Coast Guard houses, and Amtrak trains pass twice daily.

The Lighthouse Board recommended a lighthouse at Point Arguello in 1878. The following year, the landowners gave the Board fifty acres for a lighthouse station. The point's station was low on the priority list, however, and over twenty years passed before construction began.

On February 22, 1901, Keeper W.A. Beeman lit the light in a fourth-order Fresnel lens, one hundred feet above the sea. Formerly used at Point Hueneme, the lens was mounted in the small tower on the fog-signal building located on the point's outer edge. Its charateristic was fixed white. Two first class sirens operated by compressed air began blowing four months later.

A narrow land bridge connected the lighthouse with a single family dwelling and a two-story duplex. The station also had a barn and a blacksmith shop.

During the station's first years, three ships were wrecked in the area, including the *Santa Rosa.* This passenger steamship ran hard aground early on July 7, 1911, about two miles north of Point Arguello. Keeper W.A. Henderson, received a call over the wireless, and hurried to the wreck. He reported the ship, "…was lying broadside to the beach resting easy." Passengers remained aboard while two steamships tried to pull the ship free. Late in the afternoon the ship broke in two and passengers abandoned the ship. Some drowned in the surf. One man was pulled to safety by Henderson. The next day survivors walked up the hill and boarded a Southern Pacific train.

In the early 1920s newly-weds, Arvel and Helga Settles, arrived at Point Arguello. Settles was assigned as first assistant keeper. At the time only pack trails, a winding dirt road, and the train connected the station with Lompoc about twenty miles inland.

The Settles, like the other keepers and navy personnel who operated the point's new radio compass station, quickly adjusted to a self-sufficient life style. Helga planted a large garden. Crates of extra fruits and vegetables came from train crews in exchange for sacks of abalone.

For a brief time the small community was called Arlight, the contraction of Arguello and lighthouse. There was a post office, and the Settles served as postal agents. Mail sacks were thrown off the train as it rolled by. Out going mail was snatched from a metal pole. Then, "We sorted the mail on our dining room table," said Helga, who is ninety-two and lives at Friday Harbor, Washington. The Settles were at Point Arguello in 1923 when the navy suffered its worst peacetime tragedy at a place called Honda.

On the evening of September 8, a squadron of fourteen U.S. destroyers was steaming from San Francisco to San Diego at 20 knots. Near Point Arguello and in poor visibility, the lead vessel *Delphy* was receiving radio direction signals from Point Arguello's radio compass station. The ship's navigator explained that the signals placed the squadron north of the point. The squadron's commander, relying on dead reckoning, was convinced that the ships had cleared Point Conception and gave the command for a

Point Arguello's lighthouse now gone was standing in 1923 when seven destroyers sank nearby.

hard turn to the east. Within minutes, seven ships lay among the rocks north of Point Arguello.

At 10:30 p.m. keepers Gotford Olson, Settles, and Jesse Mygrants heard shouts for help. They raced to the bluff and pulled five navy men from a raft. Battered and cold, the men were treated at Olson's home.

The keepers then assisted in an all night search for other survivors. Seven ships were lost, and twenty-three men died. The keepers received commendation from the Secretary of Commerce and the navy. Today, a memorial, an anchor on a concrete pad, stands on a bluff. In waters below lay broken ships.

During the late 1920s and 1930s, old navigation aids were upgraded, new ones added, and the Point Arguello Lifeboat Station was established. In 1934 the original lighthouse was replaced by two, thirty-six inch revolving aero beacons placed on top of a forty-eight foot steel tower.

Currents, winds, fog, faulty navigation still caused shipwrecks. The *SS Harvard*, a popular passenger vessel, sailing too close to shore sliced its hull on a reef near Point Arguello the morning of May 30, 1931. All 600 aboard were safely transferred to ships that heard the *Harvard's* SOS.

According to E.D. Wheeler and R.E. Kallman in their book, *Shipwrecks, Smugglers and Maritime Mysteries,* the wreck attracted thousands of curiosity seekers who drove to the coast. The only place to park was on Adams Sykes ranch, which stretched along the bluffs. Sykes charged fifty cents for parking, and reportedly made over $10,000.

After the Coast Guard took over in 1939 more changes were made. A Loran (Long Range Navigation) station was established in 1948, the road was paved, and the keepers' quarters were remodeled into barracks. The present duplexes were built, and the lifeboat station was closed.

At one time sixteen Coast Guard personnel tended the light, fog signal, Loran and radio aids. They also continued to assist in rescues. Fishermen fell off the cliffs, pleasure boats ran out of fuel, and larger vessels wrecked on the rocks.

When the present light tower was built in 1967, the original dwellings were razed.

On July 23, 1976, Point Arguello's Officer In Charge, D.D. Larson, wrote a synopsis of the station's history for a time capsule. He concluded, "...the people that open this Bicentennial Time Capsule in 2076 should know that there was indeed an American Coast Guard Station here on south Vandenberg this date."

Point Arguello is on Vandenberg Air Force Base, and is closed to the public. However, passengers riding on Amtrak or a boat can catch a look.

Chapter 11

Anacapa Island Lighthouse

Anacapa Island is a chain of three small islets lying fourteen miles southeast of Ventura. A large rock arch juts from the sea at the eastern end of the chain. Overlooking the arch, the Anacapa Island Lighthouse beams across the Santa Barbara Channel.

In December 1853 the sidewheeler *Winfield Scott*, sailing in dense fog, went aground on the island. Bound for Panama from San Francisco, the ship carried several hundred passengers, many were successful gold seekers. All were rescued, but one survivor said, "...every one was for himself, with no thought of anything but saving his life and his (gold) dust."

A year later, James Whistler, famous for the painting of his mother, sketched Anacapa Island while working for the U.S. Coast Survey. He and other members, concluded, "It is inconceivable for a lighthouse to be constructed on this mass of volcanic rock—perpendicular on every face with an ascent inaccessible by any natural means."

Yet, others remembering the *Winfield Scott*, began to make requests to the Lighthouse Service for a lighthouse on the island. It wasn't until 1912 that the island finally received a light. It was an acetylene lens lantern on a skelton tower. Periodically, visits were made from the mainland to tend the lantern.

On March 25, 1932, the lantern was replaced by the last primary light and fog signal station to be built in California. A white, conical tower, thirty-nine feet high, stood on East Anacapa's highest point. Its revolving, third-order Fresnel lens had three panels. The light, its focal plane 277 feet above the water, could be seen up to twenty-five miles.

45

Two diaphone fog signals stood on a building near the tower. Soon after the signal went into operation, a captain reported that he heard the signal from a distance of twelve miles, stating, "In my experience at sea this is one of the best fog signals I have ever had experience with."

The station's four keepers lived in separate, Spanish-style residences. The homes were down the hill from the tower and fog signal. Each had electricty and plumbing, conveniences not yet enjoyed by keepers at other stations. The houses were connected by telephone, used mainly by the keepers' wives.

Water was supplied in part from a 30,000 square foot concrete rain catchment basin. An average rainfall of eight inches provided the station with only 18,000 gallons each year. To fill the two, 50,000 gallon redwood storage tanks, water was pumped up from tenders anchored in the cove below.

The water tanks proved to be inviting targets for people carrying guns. The practice stopped when the tanks were disguised by a frame structure designed to look like a church.

All of the station's supplies came by boat. At the time of construction, upper and lower landings had been blasted in the rock. Cranes lifted the supplies in two stages to the upper landing where the station's truck took over.

Before the lighthouse was a year old, the keeper reported a severe wind storm, estimating the easterly winds at up to eighty miles per hour. Tiles were blown from roofs and the tower's lantern became "encrusted in salt."

The keepers made regular trips to Ventura in the station's twenty-six foot cabin launch. Occasionally, when returning, high waves precluded landing, and the keepers waited out the storm anchored in the island's lee. For such emergencies, the boat was provisioned with food and water.

In 1938 Anacapa Island became a national monument to preserve its natural features and the wildlife. A year later coast guardsmen and their families moved to the island when the Coast Guard began managing lighthouses.

In 1950, a *Los Angeles Times* reporter came to the island. He wrote, "Anacapa has no water (and) no vegetation." But, the island, "Does have six Coast Guardsmen, three women and two small children. Also, two

U.S. LIGHTHOUSE SOCIETY

**Anacapa Island Lighthouse was the last major light
station to be built on the west coast.**

discouraged dogs." Because of the station's isolation, the reporter was
surprised when the residents said, "We like it. We're comfortable. We save
money."

The station was automated in 1966, and three years later Coast Guard
personnel left the island. In 1990 a rotating aero beacon replaced the
Fresnel lens. One of the three panels was given to the Channel Islands
National Park. Today, Park Service employees live in one of the remaining
Spanish-style dwellings.

Directions and Hours: Trips to the island can be arranged through the
Channel Islands National Park concessionaire in Ventura. Phone: (805)
642-1393. Early reservations are advised throughout the year.

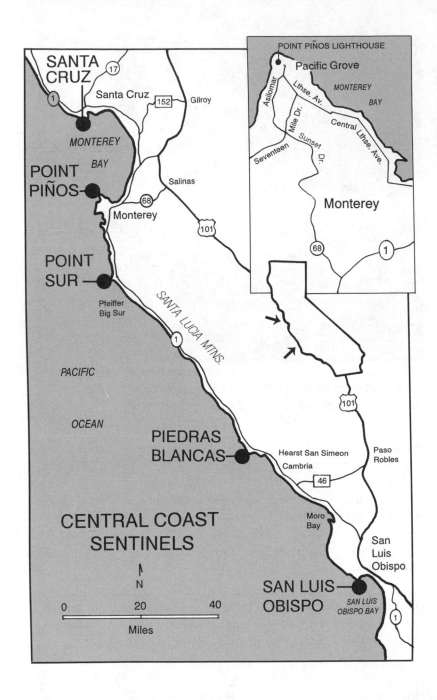

POINT PIÑOS LIGHTHOUSE

Pacific Grove

MONTEREY

BAY

Asilomar

Lthse. Av.

Mile Dr.

Central Lthse. Ave.

Seventeen

Sunset

Dr.

Monterey

68

1

SANTA
CRUZ

17

Santa Cruz

152

Gilroy

MONTEREY

BAY

POINT
PIÑOS

Salinas

68

Monterey

101

POINT
SUR

Pfeiffer
Big Sur

SANTA LUCIA MTNS.

1

101

PACIFIC

OCEAN

PIEDRAS
BLANCAS

Hearst San Simeon

Cambria

46

Paso
Robles

CENTRAL COAST
SENTINELS

Moro
Bay

San
Luis
Obispo

N

0   20   40

Miles

SAN LUIS
OBISPO

*SAN LUIS
OBISPO BAY*

1

Section 4

Central Coast Sentinels

California's central coast is dominated by the Santa Lucia Mountains. The range rises boldly from the Pacific to heights of several thousand feet, forming the backdrop for Big Sur Country. Estero Bay, with Morro Rock and Morro Bay behind, and San Luis Obispo Bay are semicircular clefts at the south end of the range. Monterey Bay lies at the range's north end.

Cabrillo explored this coast in 1542 and a Spanish galleon found shelter in Morro Bay in 1587. The Spaniard Sebastian Vizcaino came here in 1603, changing many of the geographical names given by Cabrillo.

Other explorers followed, and ships arrived to support the California Missions. Then came smugglers, fur traders, and "hiders." In 1846 American warships came up the coast to take Monterey's Presidio from Mexico. A small bay, called San Simeon once used by shore whalers, lies below the Hearst Castle.

This coast lay on the main shipping thoroughfare between San Francisco and the east, and with the gold rush, more and more ships navigated the hazardous waters. Ship wrecks became more frequent and costly, in lives and wealth lost.

Five lighthouses were built along the central coast. The Point Piños Lighthouse, on Monterey Bay, is the oldest continuosly operating lighthouse in the state. It and the Point Sur Lighthouse can be visited so they are placed first in this section. A lighthouse replica is on the site of the original Santa Cruz Lighthouse. The Piedras Blancas and San Luis Obispo lighthouses still stand but are not open to the public.

49

TED NELSON

Point Piños Lighthouse is the oldest lighthouse on the west coast and is still operating.

Chapter 12

Point Piños Lighthouse

Point Piños is the oldest, continuously operating lighthouse on the west coast. Its original, third-order Fresnel lens gleams from a tower atop the original structure. Many of the Fresnel lenses installed in west coast lighthouses in the 1800s have been lost, discarded, or replaced. The Point Piños light, however, still beams from the hand-crafted, third-order lens first lit on February 1, 1855.

Until the early 1850s the west coast was dark. There were no welcoming lights to guide mariners, and they sailed by dead reckoning. In 1852 seven lighthouses were scheduled for construction at California's hazardous headlands and active harbors, including Point Piños on Monterey Bay.

In the spring of 1853 workmen sailed from San Francisco aboard the *Oriole* to Point Piños. They quarried nearby granite to build the Cape Cod style dwelling with a tower rising through its center. This basic design was used to build most of the original west coast lighthouses.

The lighthouse was completed in 1854. Its lens came from the Fort Point Lighthouse, which was torn down shortly after it was built.

When Lighthouse Inspector Major Hartman Bache inspected the new lighthouse, he was not happy. "It answers neither the condition of a coast light or a harbor light..." he wrote. Three sites had been proposed by the Coast Survey. The contractor chose the one most inland, because, as Bache concluded, it was "...more convenient...from which to obtain the stone used in the building." This location reduced the light's arc of visibility. Today, Point Piños remains on the site selected by the contractor.

Months before the light was exhibited, the first keeper, Charles Layton, his wife, Charolette, and their four children moved into the lighthouse. Layton, an Englishman, had served in the British and United States armies. This was his first keeper's position. While the family settled into their new home, Layton rode with a posse to capture bandit, Anastacio Garcia. Layton was fatally wounded and died in November 1854.

Charolette and the children stayed on at the lighthouse. In January 1855 she was appointed keeper and days later lit the light at Point Piños, the second light to shine on the west coast. Alcatraz was the first.

Charolette tended the light until 1860 when she married George C. Harris. Then Harris took over the principal keeper's duties.

After a succession of keepers, in 1871 Allen Luce and his family moved to Point Piños. He was principal keeper, and his wife, Fannie, was his assistant.

One afternoon in 1879 a visitor from Monterey arrived at the light-house. It was Robert Louis Stevenson. His interest was more than passing. Stevenson had served as an apprentice lighthouse engineer in his father's firm, and his grandfather had originated the flashing light used in light-houses. Historian John Hussey wrote that Captain Luce was known for his hospitality and showed Stevenson the lighthouse and entertained him by playing the piano. Stevenson later wrote about Luce in the essay, "The Old Pacific Capitol."

Two years later the Luce's daughter, Erma, died in April. Luce wrote in the log, "The funeral took place from this station at 2 p.m. The Cortege was very large and consisted of the friends and relatives of the family." In October of the same year the Luces experienced a happier event. "There was born to the wife of the principal keeper, Allen Luce, at the hour 1:40 a.m. a ten pound male child."

In 1882 assistant keeper positions were abolished at several light-houses including Point Piños. Luce was ordered, "...to take Mrs. Fannie Luce off duty..." which he did.

Eleven years later Luce resigned, but not before welcoming the new keeper. On June 29, 1893, he wrote, "Mrs. E. Fish (Emily Fish), my successor arrived at the station to take charge."

Emily Fish was called, "The Socialite Keeper" by historian Clifford Gallant in an article published in the U.S. Lighthouse Society's *The Keeper's*

Log. When Emily arrived at Point Piños, she was a widow and fifty years old. With her came Que, her Chinese servant.

Born in Michigan, Emily traveled to China when she was sixteen to visit her sister and brother-in-law. While there, her sister died in childbirth leaving a daughter, Juliet. Emily married her brother-in-law, Dr. Melancthon Fish, and raised Juliet as her daughter.

Later Fish served in the Civil War, and eventually the family settled in Oakland, California. Here Emily and her husband attended theater and balls, and entertained. Then Fish died in 1891. Two years later, Emily heard from Juliet's husband, who was a lighthouse inspector, about the opening at Point Piños. She took it.

Emily quickly learned the keeper's duties, then set about to perk up the old lighthouse. She furnished it with books, paintings, and silver. Outside she and Que planted grass and trees. She purchased purebred horses and a Holstein cow.

Emily followed the keeper's routine from tending the light to escorting visitors. She kept a feather duster at the door so children could clean their shoes before entering the lighthouse. With the sun's first morning rays, she extinguished the lamp and pulled the curtains around the lens. In the watch room where she ate breakfast Que spread a linen cloth on the wide window sill and set out steaming plates of food.

Emily was a seasoned keeper when a San Francisco reporter called on her. She escorted him into the tower and told him more details than he could absorb. Showing him the lamp, she said, "...there are more things about the lamp than one would ever imagine. This is the most important thing in the house."

When not tending the light, Emily entertained writers, artists, and naval officers, and became involved in civic affairs. Often she drove to town in a "smart rig" pulled by one of her purebred horses with her French poodle trotting alongside. She headed up committees, and helped organize the Monterey-Pacific Grove American Red Cross.

On April 18, 1906, Emily recorded in the log, "At 5:30 a.m. violent and continued earthquake shocks jarred the lens causing it to bend the connecting tube and loosened the lens, so it was unstable, also enlarged the crack in the tower...the water in the wood house tank was thrown on the floor." It was two days before she and Que received news of the destruction in San Francisco.

Though the tower was badly damaged, the lens survived. A year later a new tower of the same design was built of reinforced concrete, and the lens was placed in working order.

In 1914 Emily retired at age seventy-one. Days before she left Point Piños she received a letter of Commendation from the Department of Commerce. Then she and Que moved into her recently purchased home in Pacific Grove. Que later returned to China. Emily died in 1931.

Electricity came to Point Pinos in 1915. Eleven years later a fog signal was installed. Neighbors accustomed to peace and quiet objected. Over the years different signals were tried to satisfy both fishermen and neighbors, but still there were complaints. One woman said the signal caused convulsions in her dog. A hotel owner offered to sell his property "cheap" to the government.

In 1939 two veteran Lighthouse Service keepers, George F. Petersen and Tom Henderson and families moved to Point Piños. That same year a new dwelling was built, and the Coast Guard assumed management of lighthouses. Both men chose to continue their light keeping duties as civilians. Petersen retired in 1953 and Henderson in 1955.

In 1975 the lighthouse was automated, and licensed to the Pacific Grove Historical Society. They restored the old lighthouse, furnished it with antiques, and set-up interpretive displays. When you visit the lighthouse you will be welcomed by Bruce J. Handy, Keeper of the Light since 1983. You can also see the watch room, where Que once spread a linen cloth to serve Emily's breakfast.

Directions and Hours: From Highway 1 in Monterey turn west onto State Route 68. Follow it to Sunset Drive then to Asilomar Avenue. Turn right onto Asilomar and follow it to the lighthouse. It is open Saturday and Sunday from 1 P.M. to 4 P.M.

Chapter 13

Point Sur Lighthouse

An article in the April 1992 issue of *Sunset* quotes Juan Rodriguez Cabrillo's journals as he sailed by the Big Sur country in 1542. "All the coast passed this day is very bold, there is a great swell and the land is very high. There are numerous mountains which seem to reach the heavens and the sea beats against them."

The article then quotes Jack Kerouac, the poet of the "sixties" after a trip to Big Sur. He contemplated the area's, "...reputation of being beautiful above and beyond its fearfulness..." Cabrillo had come by caravel from Navidad, Mexico. Kerouac had come by taxi from San Francisco. Today, three million visitors come to the area via Highway 1.

In 1874 the Lighthouse Board had a more pragmatic view of the Big Sur country and Point Sur in particular. The point was described as an important landmark to mariners, but the nearest seacoast lights were at Piedras Blancas to the south and Pigeon Point to the north, each about sixty miles distant. The Board said that there should be a lighthouse on the point but, "...the erection there of a lighthouse, with the accompanying buildings, will be an expensive project."

Much of the cost would be required to prepare the site before the first stone could be laid. The steep, island-like point was 369 feet high. Its top was only ten to twelve feet wide. Around much of the wedge shaped point, the rock faces were almost vertical. A stretch of soft sand connected the point to the main coastal headlands.

The steamship *Ventura* was lost near the point in 1875, but it wasn't until 1886 that the first appropriation for the lighthouse was approved. By

55

then, the Board estimated that the eventual cost would be at least $100,000.

Preconstruction work began in May 1887 when materials were, "...safely landed through heavy surf..." A quarry was established on the mainland to provide granite for the buildings. A railway, over seven hundred feet long, climbed 318 feet up the point's landward side. One section had thirty-seven trestles.

On the seaward face, a road-bed was blasted out and nearly five hundred feet of track was laid to the tower's site, 272 feet above the surf. The narrow ridge was leveled away to accommodate the main dwelling and out buildings. More blasting was required for the cistern and a corduroy road was laid across the sand to the mainland.

Construction of the buildings then began and by November 1888 the station was nearly complete. The forty-foot granite tower, with adjoining rooms for fuel storage and steam whistle boilers, stood ready to receive its lens. Most of the outside stone work on the keepers' dwelling was finished, and the fog-signal apparatus was in place. Then, work was discontinued. The $100,000 spent.

Work resumed with a new appropriation in the spring of 1889, and on August 1 the light was shown from a first-order Fresnel lens. It gave alternating, red and white flashes at fifteen second intervals.

Three keepers were housed in a triplex building and a fourth keeper was assigned to a small building left over from construction. A shed, later converted to a keeper's dwelling, housed a donkey engine used to winch supplies up the railway.

A barn was soon built at the base of the railway and fences put up around the dwellings to, "... prevent the keepers' children from falling off."

The fence was held in good stead by Cora Isabel Owens. She had come to the point with her husband, Bill, when he was assigned as an assistant keeper in 1935. The Owens had five children. Writing in *The Keeper's Log*, she recalled the cramped space in the triplex when they first arrived from Point Conception. But she wrote, "Soil had been brought in so each family could have a small garden. Also, there was a small patch in front of each assistant's quarters for flowers. Mr. Henderson, the head keeper, even managed to find room for a cow."

The Owens' older children were now able to attend school after being taught by their mother at Point Conception. "Miss Gilbert was the teacher, she gave our two girls extra lessons in each subject." The girls walked down the steep road built in 1900 and across the corduroy road. Of the nine students, four were from the lighthouse. The school had been built by the U.S. government, and the teacher was paid by the county.

A month before the Owens came to Point Sur, Keeper Henderson had witnessed the loss of the navy's dirigible, the *Macon*. It was the second time that a lighter-than-air craft fell near the point. In 1903, according to the *Monterey Peninsula Hearld*, the gas ballon *Dr.Greth Mammoth Air Liner* was launched from San Francisco's Market Street to promote air travel. It was supposed to circle the bay and return. Instead, the ballon was blown south. "After hours of silence a telegram from the Point Sur Lighthouse keeper told (of the pilots) disheveled arrival on foot."

The loss of the *Dr. Greth* was humorous except to the promoters. The loss of the *Macon* was tragic. On the evening of February 12, 1935, Keeper Henderson was preparing his light for the night. "Through glasses" he watched the 785-foot long *Macon* flying abreast of the point in rain squalls. Four biplanes were tucked inside the airborne hanger. In a later inquiry, Keeper Henderson said, "...the fin seemed to go to pieces very suddenly. The fabric drifted back..." The airship fell to the water, floated for about forty minutes, then sank. Two of the crew of eighty-three were lost.

The lighthouse was automated in 1972, and two rotating aero beacons were placed in the lantern room. The first-order lens, is now on display at Monterey's Stanton Center.

The Point Sur lighthouse station remains much like it was when first built. Docents with California's Department of Parks and Recreation lead regular hiking tours up to the tower and to the dwellings above.

A quote in the Work Projects Administration's California Guidebook still rings true. When one of the original workers was asked what he thought of the light, he said, "Good light, but she no work. Go all the time sad, 'Boo-Boo,' but the fog, she creep in just the same."

Directions and Hours: Lighthouse tours are given every Sunday at 10 A.M. and 1 P.M. Each tour accommodates forty people on a first come, first serve basis. The tours start at the gate to the point from Highway 1 about twenty-five miles south of Monterey. Moonlight tours are also conducted. Phone: (408) 625-4419. The Stanton Center is in Monterey at 5 Custom House Plaza. Open daily, except Mondays and national holidays, the hours vary. Phone: (408) 373-2469.

TED NELSON

Point Sur light station has changed little since it began operating in 1889.

Chapter 14

San Luis Obispo Lighthouse

Driving through San Luis Obispo on Highway 101 there is little hint of the area's early maritime history. Between 1914 and 1922 San Luis Obispo was the largest shipper of crude oil in the world. Long before, in 1876 the *San Luis Obispo Tribune* engaged in an editorial debate over the *Santa Barbara Daily Press*'s "...attempts to annihilate San Luis Obispo Harbor." The *Tribune* questioned the *Press's* use of the tales of old otter hunters and old Spanish and Russian charts in a "senseless attack" on San Luis Obispo.

The *Tribune* quoted Captain Stoddard of the steamer *Senator* after he had been blown off his anchorage at Santa Barbara. He said, "If I had been in San Luis...I could have landed my freight and passengers ...and not had to anchor to weather the storm."

At the time of this debate, Santa Barbara had a lighthouse. San Luis Obispo did not. But, San Luis Obispo had John Harford's long wharf extending into the bay not far from where the San Luis Obispo Lighthouse would eventually stand. The port was then called Port Harford. It was known for its shipments of fruits and grain. In a twelve month period covering 1885 and 1886, 423 steamers and 30 lumber schooners arrived at the dock.

About this time the Lighthouse Board began extolling the virtues of the Port and the need for a lighthouse there. The 1885 Board Report said, "...The bay of San Luis Obispo is the most important roadstead on the Pacific coast south of San Francisco, and with one exception is also the best."

Appropriations for a light and fog signal were made in 1887, but after that progress was slow. There was a delay in acquiring the property on San Luis Head near Avila Beach. Then the first bids were too high, and the project had to be rebid. In 1888, according to historian Mark Hall-Patton, impetus was added for a lighthouse when the steamer *Queen of the Pacific* sank while trying to reach the port in darkness.

When the completion date of December 15, 1889, arrived, the work was only half finished, and the contractor's bondsman had to take over. In the meantime, the Pacific Coast Steamship Company employed a Portugese fisherman to keep a light and fire a gun over an offshore shoal in foggy weather.

The station was finally completed in May 1890, and the lamp was first lit on June 30, 1890. The fourth-order Fresnel lens showed alternating red and white flashes, its focal plane 133 feet above the water.

The light shone from a square, frame tower attached to the corner of a Victorian dwelling. An assistant keepers' dwelling stood nearby on the then treeless slope. There was a steam fog-signal building with two smoke stacks and a rain catchment basin feeding a 100,000 gallon cistern. A small wharf lay east of the station for handling supplies.

Unlike many other stations, San Luis Obispo's buildings were little affected by earthquakes and storms. But since rainfall was inadequate to service the fog signal a three and one-half mile pipeline had to be laid to a small dam on Pecho Creek. The water system remained troublesome. Also, the wharf required periodic repair. In 1892 it was strengthened and extended. The *Tribune* reported that the new timbers were being prepared with, "...Capt. Cass' famed teredo-proof oinment..."

In 1892 the the paper also reported that, "The government's light house supply steamer, *Madrona*, departed this morning, having left coal and general supplies at the light house. Capt. Young, with Mr. Souza and the irrepressible Ballou, keep everything in and about the light house shining...and the inspector was immensely pleased with their conduct of the government's property."

A 1917 "Description of Light Station" described access to the station as by boat or foot path and, "...Also by wagon road but the road is steep and rough." Little had changed long after the Coast Guard had taken over the lighthouse. In 1962 Coast Guard inspector Capt. V. C. Gibson de-

San Luis Obispo Lighthouse may one day be open to the public.

scribed a road built in the 1950s as not qualifying, "...as a road in any sense. A jeep is the only small passenger vehicle... capable of traversing this route."

By that time new Coast Guard quarters had been built and the assistant keepers' dwelling razed. In 1974 the station was automated. Two rotating aero beacons were placed on a low tower on the point, and in 1976 the Fresnel lens was moved to the San Luis Obispo County Historical Museum. The original keeper's dwelling with its tower and the fog-signal building remained. A new chapter for the lighthouse began.

In 1978 the Port of San Luis Harbor District gained a license from the Coast Guard to restore the lighthouse. The District stopped vandalism at the site and stabilized the buildings' condition. Since that time, the port, community leaders, federal agencies, the San Luis Obispo Land Conservancy, and the Pacific Gas and Electric Company, who owns the nearby Diablo Canyon nuclear facility, have worked to restore the light station and to make it accessible to the public.

Events in 1992 moved these efforts forward when ownership of the lighthouse was transferred to the San Luis Obispo Harbor Commission. Also, the Nature Conservancy started a seven-mile Pecho Coast Hike which passes the lighthouse.

Soon others, like the hikers, may be able to visit the station as a reminder of the days San Luis Obispo Bay was condidered, "...the most important roadstead on the Pacific coast south of San Francisco..."

Directions and Hours: The County Museum is located at 696 Monterey Street in San Luis Obispo. Open Wednesday through Sunday, 10 A.M. to 4 P.M. Phone: (805) 543-0638. For current information on the status of this or other lighthouses, write the U.S. Lighthouse Society, 244 Kearny Street, 5th Floor, San Francisco, California, 94108.

Chapter 15

Piedras Blancas Lighthouse

Seen today, though its top is gone, the tall Piedras Blancas tower still appears like an early, classic sea coast tower. Three such towers were built in California in the 1870s. Point Arena's was replaced, while Pigeon Point, and Piedras Blancas remain. These classic towers, well-known on the east coast lowlands, were seldom needed on the west coast with its high cliffs and headlands.

Piedras Blancas, a low point jutting seaward north of San Simeon, was chosen as a lighthouse site in the early 1870s. Until then there were no guiding lights between Point Conception to the south and Point Piños to the north—a gap of over 150 miles.

In April 1874 material for the new tower was, "...landed through the surf." Shanties were built for the workmen, then blasting began to level a rocky knob for the lighthouse foundation. In late fall the 115-foot tall tower was completed. The base walls were five feet thick and tapered to eighteen inches at the parapet. Little remained of the $75,000 appropriation, and neither the fog signal nor the keepers' dwelling were built.

Regardless, the first keepers moved into the workmen's shanties and lit the lamp's five wicks in the first-order Fresnel lens on February 15, 1875. Before the next rainy season, the three keepers and their families moved into a new two-story, Victorian-style dwelling.

The lens, made in 1872, weighed several tons and rotated quietly, easily on chariot wheels. A clockwork mechanism with heavy weights was wound every hour to rotate the lens. In 1880 large birds flew into the lantern panes shattering glass that chipped the lens.

One of the first keepers was Captain Lorin Thorndyke, who was a seasoned mariner and had circumnavigated the globe several times. He was promoted to principal keeper in 1881. The Thorndyke sons, Lorin and Emory, were born at the lighthouse. In 1885 Mrs. Thorndyke died. Though a widower with young sons to raise, Thorndyke stayed on.

Several times a year the tender delivered supplies to the point's small wharf: flour, staples, and coal for the families; kerosene, wicks, and cleaning rags for the lighthouse. When deliveries arrived on thick, foggy days, Lorin marveled at how the tender's captain found the wharf without mishap.

In 1906 a fog-signal and a new dwelling for a fourth keeper were built. The fog-signal building still stands about two hundred feet seaward from the tower.

Capt. Thorndyke, who was seventy-five and looking for an excuse to retire, claimed the fog-signal noise bothered him, and he retired the same year.

In 1934 Norman Leo Francis and his family arrived at Piedras Blancas. Francis had served at Point Reyes, Point Arguello, and Los Angeles Harbor twice. Each time he was promoted, and he arrived at Piedras Blancas as principal keeper.

Francis joined the Lighthouse Service after answering an ad. To qualify for a light keeper's position he had to pass several tests; trim a wick, saw a square cut on a 1x12 inch board, and lift two sacks of coal at the same time onto a platform.

His new assignment in some ways was a step backwards. Their previous home had electric lights. At Piedras Blancas, the family used kerosene lamps, and coal for heating and cooking. The family quickly adjusted. Son, Norman, described his father as a "happy lighthouse keeper." When it was his time to stand watch, Francis climbed the tower's spiral stairs singing loudly in an "off-key tenor voice."

Norman was eleven at the time, and his sister, Lenore, was ten. They lived in the 1906 dwelling. Norman helped polish the brass on the lens, and eventually, his father let him clean the lens.

Norman's appreciation of the first-order Fresnel lens with its many prisms began when his father took him up into the lantern room one summer day. His father raised a shade that protected the lens from the sun's rays. The exposed lens reflected and refracted the rays and filled the lantern room with rainbow lights. "It was beautiful," said Norman.

Piedras Blancas light tower as it looked before the lens and lantern were removed.

In a newspaper interview, Norman also told how living near the Hearst's San Simeon Castle later proved to be an extra bonus. When William Randolph Hearst and guests arrived, high school students, including Norman, worked at the castle. They stayed in the servants' quarters for two weeks. They arose early in the morning, washed dishes, carried guests' luggage, and occasionally caught a glimpse of Hearst, Erroll Flynn, and Marion Davies.

Francis continued to tend the Piedras Blancas light after the Coast Guard took over in 1939. He retired in 1948.

A year later a storm damaged the lantern room. The Coast Guard removed it and the lens, capped the tower, and placed a rotating aero beacon on top.

For a brief time, the lens lay in pieces scattered about in a field, then the Cambria Lions Club rescued it. They reassembled the lens and placed it on display outdoors near the Veterans Hall. Later, the 1906 dwelling was sold, moved, and restored as a home in Cambria.

In 1960 the Coast Guard razed the original dwelling, and built four homes for Coast Guard keepers and their families. While they tended the Piedras Blancas light, they printed informative pamphlets and conducted tours. This ceased when Piedras Blancas was automated in 1975 and no longer needed the care of human hands. Three years later the station was leased to the U.S. Fish and Wildlife Service. Today, marine biologists walk beneath the "decapitated" sea coast tower.

A few years ago, concern about the first-order Frensel lens and its exposure to weather began to mount. The brass frames holding the prisms were tarnished. The prisms had lost their luster.

Norman Francis returned to Cambria after a career with the Central Intelligence Agency. Remembering the brilliant sun-lit lens of his youth, he with Lion Club members began a campaign to restore the lens. Many talks and letters later, they watched on a summer day in 1990 while Coast Guard personnel disassembled the lens and took it to Monterey to be restored. A month later Francis died.

In the fall of 1992 Friends of Piedras Blancas Light built a lantern room replica to shelter the lens. Now the restored lens, appearing as it did when Francis saw it that summer day, can be seen at Pinedorado Grounds on Main Street in Cambria.

The Piedras Blancas station is closed to the public, but can be seen from Highway 1.

Chapter 16

Santa Cruz Lighthouse

"This lighthouse seems more like a country home than a Government station." This was a writer's observation of the Santa Cruz Lighthouse in the late 1800s. Cypress trees grew behind the lighthouse. Flowers bordered the walkways. A large vegetable garden grew in the sideyard. Still, the light was meticulously cared for by its keeper, Miss Laura Heacox.

The Santa Cruz light station was one of the ideal stations to tend. There was no fog signal with an appetite for coal. It was close to town, and most of the time the weather was mild. Today, the original lighthouse is gone; a memorial lighthouse stands in its place.

In the early 1850s money was appropriated and plans moved ahead to build a lighthouse at the north side of Monterey Bay on Point Santa Cruz. Before construction could begin the site had to be purchased, and land title entanglements led to a delay. All the while, more ships sailed into busy Santa Cruz harbor to take on redwood lumber, lime, and agricultural products.

In 1868 title problems were resolved, and a year later the Lighthouse Board reported that the Santa Cruz Lighthouse, "...will be a duplicate of that at Ediz Hook, W.T. (Washington Territory). It consists of a wooden dwelling on a brick foundation...and surmounted by a wooden tower for the lantern and lens."

The first keeper, A.A. Heacox, his wife, and their fourteen-year-old daughter, Laura, moved into the lighthouse, and Heacox lit the lamp on December 31, 1869. The light, fixed white, beamed from a fifth-order Fresnel lens.

Several years later more residential lights appeared near the point creating "light noise." Mariners had a difficult time distinguishing the tower's light from other lights. The characteristic was changed to fixed red by replacing the lamp's clear glass chimney with one tinted red.

Heacox was a former clergyman who had also served in Santa Cruz's local politics. He was sixty-four when he became keeper. This was a one keeper station. But, when extra help was needed he could rely on Laura. She trimmed the wicks and cleaned the lamp chimneys. She enjoyed living near the sea, and in her spare time wandered the beaches and collected shells.

Heacox was seventy-three and still serving as keeper when it became apparent the low bluff where the lighthouse stood was being undermined by the sea. The lighthouse was jacked onto rollers, and pulled inland by horses. Even in transit, the light was lit each night.

After Heacox died in 1883, Laura was assigned keeper. She and her mother continued to live at the lighthouse.

As Laura tended to her duties, she wore a large keeper's apron over her long dress with long sleeves. Her dark hair was pulled back in a chignon.

In 1895 a reporter from San Francisco came to see how Laura managed in a world seemingly reserved for men. He was impressed. "The worry and care of keeping the light is bad enough," he wrote, "but the daily attendance on it is an added strain. There are rules for the ceremony of lighting it, and rules for the ceremony of putting it out...and more rules for keeping it clean and free from dust."

Nevertheless, this did not diminish Laura's pleasure in her work, which she felt was important. "It's good to fall asleep," she told the reporter, "with that light burning so steadfastly above my head, warning the mariner from death and peril, and with the sound of the whistling bouy and the surf in my ears."

Laura's shell collection continued to grow. Wanting to share it with visitors, she labelled the shells and displayed them in one of the lighthouse rooms. Later, Laura bequeathed her collection to the city with the stipulation that the city start a museum. It did.

During the 1906 earthquake, the Santa Cruz Lighthouse suffered little damage compared to its southern neighbor, Point Piños. As told by Frank Perry in his book, *Lighthouse Point,* only the lamp's chimney was shattered, and Laura quickly reacted to keep the lamp burning.

In 1909 the Lighthouse Board recommended the station be upgraded with a modern lens and a fog signal. A fourth-order lens was installed, but plans for the fog signal were dropped.

Laura's mother died at the lighthouse in 1908, and Laura retired in 1916. Thus, ended forty-six years of the Heacox family tending the Santa Cruz Lighthouse.

One more keeper, Arthur Anderson, served at the lighthouse, until it was discontinued in 1941. An automated minor light was placed on a wood scaffolding seaward of the original lighthouse. During World War II, the Coast Guard used the tower as a coastal lookout. In 1948 the lighthouse was razed, and the light on the scaffold stood alone until twenty years later.

In 1965 Mark Abbott, an eighteen-year-old, was surfing near the point and drowned. His parents, Chuck and Esther Abbott decided to use Mark's insurance money to build a lighthouse as a memorial to their son. "We had $20,000 and no Mark," Mrs. Abbott told a reporter, "We wanted to do something with it that would please Mark. Our family had always loved lighthouses, so we decided that was the best thing we could do."

The brick lighthouse was completed in 1967 near the site of the original. Its lantern room is from the Oakland Harbor Lighthouse. Inside the lantern the Coast Guard installed and maintains an operating optic.

It is now the Santa Cruz Surfing Museum. Lighthouse paintings, an historical display, and a small gift shop are on the main floor. A plaque reads: "Mark Abbott, age 18, challenged the sea and lost, Feb. 28, 1965."

Directions and Hours: Museum hours are noon to 4 P.M. Closed Tuesdays. From the Santa Cruz Beach Broadwalk follow West Cliff Drive. Phone: (408) 429-3429.

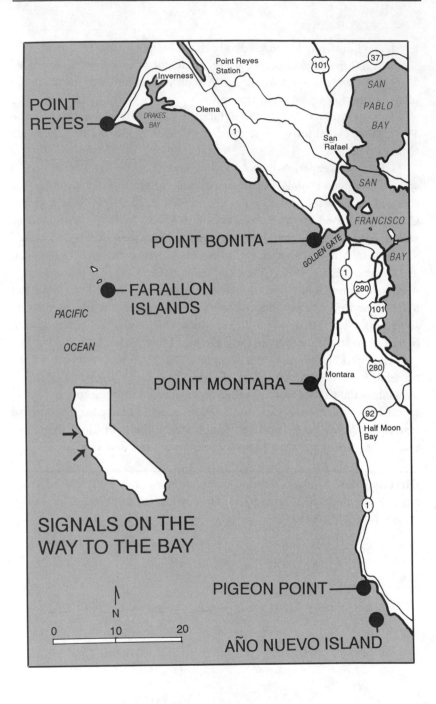

POINT
REYES

POINT BONITA

FARALLON
ISLANDS

PACIFIC

OCEAN

POINT MONTARA

SIGNALS ON THE
WAY TO THE BAY

PIGEON POINT

AÑO NUEVO ISLAND

N

0   10   20

Point Reyes
Station

Inverness

DRAKES
BAY

Olema

San
Rafael

SAN
PABLO
BAY

SAN

FRANCISCO

GOLDEN GATE

BAY

Montara

Half Moon
Bay

Section 5

Signals on the Way to the Bay

The 1869 *Coast Pilot* gave careful sailing directions for approaching San Fransico Bay. The first advice was, "In approaching the land in the vicinity of San Francisco, it is of great importance that accurate determinations of their vessel's position should often be obtained by shipmasters, as fogs and thick weather are apt to prevail near the land."

For vessels coming from the southward, the *Coast Pilot* stated, "...it is customary to make the coast about Point Año Nuevo and then to follow it up to the bar..." From the west mariners were advised to, "...sight South Farallon lighthouse..." leaving it to the north. The approach from the northwest began at Point Reyes. Upon nearing the bay, mariners were advised to look for the Point Bonita Lighthouse (the first one) its white tower, "...projected against the high, dark hills behind..." This headland marked the north entrance to the Golden Gate.

The *Coast Pilot* stated, "The Golden Gate is the entrance to the bay, and presents the character of a great cleft or fissure in the sea-coast mountains thereby connecting the bay of San Francisco with the Pacific Ocean."

By 1875 four more stations had been established to aid mariners along this busy approach to the bay, including Point Año Nuevo, Pigeon Point, and Points Montara and Reyes. The San Francisco lightship was stationed near the bay's entrance in 1898.

U.S. LIGHTHOUSE SOCIETY

Año Nuevo Island light station is now the home of elephant seals and sea lions.

Chapter 17

Año Nuevo Island Lighthouse

Originally, Año Nuevo Island Lighthouse was a fog signal station operated by two keepers—the first such station in California. The island, nine acres of clay and sand, is located one-half mile off Point Año Nuevo and six miles south of Pigeon Point. Today, it is part of Año Nuevo State Reserve.

Also called New Year's Island, it has long held an affinity for mammals. With the first blast of the steam whistle on May 29, 1872, cows from a neighboring dairy ranch stampeded to the beach. The rancher commented, "The cows must have thought there was a very wonderful bull down there." Years later, Keeper Otto Becker complained that the growing sea lion rookery was over-running his house. A killer whale had frightened the young sea lions, and they forced their way into each room.

The station was abandoned in 1948. Everything was left in place. Today, the light tower lies on its side, sea lions occupy the dwellings, and elephant seals breed on the island.

As the Lighthouse Service was lighting the west coast, dark stretches still remained. One, nearly ninety miles long, between Monterey Bay and the Golden Gate included Point Año Nuevo and Pigeon Point. Each had been considered a site for a light station. Difficulty in securing land title led to delays.

In the meantime, ships were wrecked and lives lost on the rocks near Point Año Nuevo and Pigeon Point. Irate citizens and newspaper editors demanded a lighthouse. In 1868, $90,000 was appropriated for a first-order lighthouse at "Point Año Nuevo or vicinity." Both Año Nuevo Island and Pigeon Point were held by the same owners. They were asking an "extravagant sum" for a site. In 1869, a frustrated Lighthouse Board received an offer from another owner for land on Point Año Nuevo. The island's owners, fearing they would lose out, accepted $10,000 for both Año Nuevo Island and Pigeon Point.

Titles secured, the Lighthouse Service proceeded to build a lighthouse and fog signal at Pigeon Point and a fog signal on Año Nuevo Island. By May 1872 a twelve-inch steam whistle was operating at Año Nuevo. The fog-signal building stood near one end of the island. A wooden walkway connected the fog signal with the keepers' dwelling on the other end. A rain catchment basin supplied water for the station.

Getting on and off the island was never an easy row. Waves washed around the island and clashed on the landward side creating a rough and sometimes deadly passage.

One Sunday in April 1883 two brothers from a neighboring farm left the island at 2:30 p.m. They were accompanied by the keepers. Mid-way, breakers swamped the boat, turned it over, and all were washed out to sea. The keepers' wives watched, horrified. Though a clear day, the women fired up the fog signal, and flew the flag upside down—signals of distress to hail passing ships.

The steamer, *Los Angeles* responded. Crewmen searched but found nothing. The next day J.L. Ryan, first assistant keeper at Pigeon Point, arrived to help. He found the widows, "Wild with Grief." Ryan took charge. He was later assigned as principal keeper on the island.

Ryan, as with keepers before and after him, found the seals and sea lions bothersome. One keeper said, "The smell and the noise of them. I never thought I'd get used to it." Still, the keepers tried to protect them. Thomas Owen, on June 4, 1879, wrote, "The Capt and crew of the schooner, *New York*, landed on the island for the purpose of killing seals." Owen told the men to leave. They refused. Seal hunters also defied Keeper Ryan's orders to stop.

In 1890 a lens lantern was mounted on a water tank. By 1906 a two-story duplex was built next to the original dwelling. In 1915 a skeleton tower with a watch room, lantern room, and a Fresnel lens replaced the lens lantern. The lens was shattered in a 1926 earthquake, and the lens lantern was used again until a new lens could be installed.

In 1929 young Radford Franke arrived from San Francisco for his first lighthouse assignment. He came by motorcoach and got off at the roadside. Carrying a suitcase he hiked a mile and a half across ranchland and sand dunes. As he stood on the beach, sand blowing in his face and waiting for the keeper to arrive in the dory, Franke wondered what he was getting into.

There was no electricity. Three keepers lived at the station, but, ususally there were only two. The island was "isolated duty," and each keeper received ninety-six days annual vacation. Work days were long, but Franke liked it, and wrote to Marie, his wife, to join him. The Frankes lived in the upstairs of the duplex.

"We had to be careful about the water," said Franke. "If we ran short, the women would have to leave, and water would be brought by tender." They used it sparingly, and watered the few vegetables they grew with bath water.

While the Frankes lived on the island one of the keepers brewed beer in his quarters. One day, without warning, the tender steamed towards the island the inspector's flag flying. The keeper acted quickly. The inspector, who usually inspected everything, passed by the brewing room. Its floor was wet with fresh paint.

Eighteen months after arriving at Año Nuevo Island, Franke was transferred to Ballast Point.

The station was closed in May 1948. Vessel traffic patterns had changed, and electronics served ships during fog. An automatic light and sound buoy replaced the station.

Directions and Hours: The island can be seen but not visited on guided walks during elephant seal breeding season, December to March. For reservations phone: 1-800-444-7275. To walk a beach trail, obtain a permit at the reserve entrance just off Highway 1. Hours are 8 A.M. to 4 P.M. Phone: (415)-879-0227.

TED NELSON

Pigeon Point's classic sea coast tower was recently refurbished.

Chapter 18

Pigeon Point Lighthouse

In an early 1900s edition the *Coast Pilot,* usually staid in its style, described Pigeon Point for mariners, its rocky bluff and rocks lying offshore. It then added, "Pigeon Point was named for the wreck at this place (1853) of the Clippership *Carrier Pigeon.*" Not a comforting thought. But by then, the fog signal and the light were in place, and coasting ships that some times passed within a mile of Pigeon Point had signals to warn them of the dangers.

Today, the Pigeon Point Lighthouse, a 115-foot tall tower, is the best example in California of a classic sea coast tower. Of the three built in the 1870s, including Piedras Blancas and Point Arena, Pigeon Point remains unchanged. Its original first-order lens is still in the lantern room. The chariot wheels on which the lens turned are still there, but no longer function. An automated aero beacon now serves as the light.

In the mid-1850s when the Lighthouse Board was selecting more lighthouse sites, both Pigeon Point and Point Año Nuevo, six miles south, were considered. One report favored Pigeon Point, because "...It is four miles westward...and has a larger visibility sector." Yet, no decision was made, and the Civil War intervened.

In 1865 and 1866 two shipwrecks and the loss of many lives near Pigeon Point increased public pressure to build a lighthouse and fog signal in the area. In 1868 $90,000 was appropriated for a first-order light at "Point Año Nuevo or vicinity."

77

Two years later, the Lighthouse Board purchased the island off Point Año Nuevo, and "One and one-half acres of the extreme tip of Pigeon Point, (and) nine acres about one-third mile inland for water privileges..."

Construction at the point began in late spring 1871. The fog-signal building and Victorian four-plex dwelling were completed first. The twelve-inch steam whistle began operation September 10, 1871.

Since the point was low, a tall tower was needed to increase the light's range, and plans for a North Carolina coastal lighthouse were used for Pigeon Point. Due to construction problems, bad weather, and late delivery of the lantern and lens, the light was not exhibited until November 15, 1872.

Stories vary about the lens' origin. But, according to a letter written in 1924 by George R. Putnam, Commissioner of Lighthouses, the Pigeon Point lens "...appears to be the second lens placed in commission at the Cape Hatteras L.S. (North Carolina)." When a new (and the present) Cape Hatteras tower was built in 1870, the lens was removed from the old tower and later shipped to Pigeon Point.

A local story tells that while tower builders worked, smells of boiling whale blubber and decaying carcasses probably drifted their way from the whaling village east of the point. The men were glad to finish.

An oil storage room and workroom are located at the tower's base. Both rooms have fireplaces which kept the keepers warm and helped keep the tower's interior dry.

Routines for the four keepers were like other light stations. An exception at Pigeon Point was the need to haul gallons of lamp fuel up the 147 steps, the equivalent of an eleven-story building. Most stations used coal for the fog-signal boilers, but Pigeon Point used wood. In 1888 keepers stoked the boilers with ninety-four cords to operate the steam whistle 1067 hours.

Years later the fog signal led to the wreck of the *Columbia* on July 14, 1896. The ship was on a run from Panama to San Francisco, and the captain, trying to set a speed record, ignored the fog and kept the ship at top speed. Near Pigeon Point he heard the station's fog signal, and thinking it was a ship's signal steered his ship to avoid a collision. He ran onto the rocks instead. No lives were lost. Residents from Pescadero salvaged the cargo, and the ship eventually broke apart.

Frank Perry in *The History of Pigeon Point*, included an additional note about the wreck. Keeper James Marner was on duty when he heard the *Columbia* hit. Thinking that it was the tender dropping anchor and the inspector was on board, Marner, "...hollared to the boys, and they ran to put their good clothes on to receive the inspector, but we found our mistake."

The light guided ships at sea, and one night in 1911 it guided a rowboat to safety. Officers and crew abandoned their motor schooner after it struck an object thirteen miles at sea. They rowed all night using the Pigeon Point light to reach the shore.

The light too led to a mishap. When the Coast Guard tended the station, a wet skipper and crew appeared at the lighthouse at 4 a.m. The skipper had been lost and thought the tower's light was a ship's light. Sailing his yacht toward the light to ask directions, he hit the rocks.

The Victorian dwelling was torn down in 1960, and four new Coast Guard homes were built. A few years later the aero beacon replaced the rotating lens. The station was automated in 1974 and vacated. Vandals, however, caused havoc, so the Coast Guard assigned a caretaker.

Seaman Albert S. Tucker, who requested the duty, and his wife moved to Pigeon Point in 1977. Intruders continued to come. People stopped to use the phone or bathroom, and a fisherman used the Tucker's grill to cook his fresh caught fish.

The Tuckers bought a Doberman, but uninvited sigthseers were not fazed by the dog. Tucker bought a young pig and named it Lester who grew to about eight hundred pounds. "With his good-sized tusks, nobody came in with him here," said Tucker.

While at the station, Tucker maintained the navigational aids and conducted tours, and unhappy with the condition of the lighthouse, he also chipped old paint and applied new. One day while working in the lantern room atop the tower, he heard something on the stairs. It kept coming. When Tucker looked up, he saw Lester, the pig.

In December 1979 Tucker received an achievement award from the Coast Guard for his accomplishments at Pigeon Point. A few months later the Coast Guard licensed the station, except an oil-storage building and the lighthouse, to the California Department of Parks and Recreation. The 1900 fog-signal building and Coast Guard homes are now used by American Youth Hostels to accommodate overnight travelers.

Until mid-1992 the Año Nuevo Interpretive Association led tours through the lighthouse. Later, the Coast Guard restored the tower, and it is expected that it will be reopened for tours.

Directions and Hours: Pigeon Point Lighthouse is on Highway 1 nineteen miles south of Half Moon Bay. For current tour information call the American Youth Hostel (415) 879-0633.

Chapter 19

Point Montara Lighthouse

Point Montara, about twenty miles south of San Francisco, is a southern spur of Montara mountain. According to the *Coast Pilot,* "It terminates in cliffs about 60 feet with numerous out lying rocks... a dangerous locality in thick weather." For early mariners who sailed close to the coast as they approached the Golden Gate, the area in "thick weather" was especially hazardous. At the time a fog signal would be more useful than a light.

On March 1, 1875, a twelve-inch steam whistle began operation on the point. Nearby a Victorian duplex, which still stands, housed the two keepers and their families. This was the third fog-signal station established in California. It was preceded by Año Nuevo Island and Yerba Buena Island.

The keepers were kept busy. Fog could last for days requiring them constantly to stoke the boilers and tend the signal. Point Montara was often fog-bound the equivalent of forty or more days each year.

In 1880 George Koons replaced W.A. Price as principal keeper. Koons was not pleased with Price nor the condition of the station. He wrote in the log on September 9, "Price was invited to resign for cursing the government that gave him a living. The miserable little Irish rebel..." Koons found the boiler had not been cleaned, "...from the time it was put in, as I was compelled to take a sledge hammer to arrive at a hand hold..." A month later, Koons feeling calmer, wrote, "From now on, nothing but work, cleaning, building, making garden."

By 1882 a duplicate whistle as back up had been installed, and the

Lighthouse Board reported, "The boilers and machinery were thoroughly overhauled and repaired and are now in good condition."

A light was established at the point twenty-five years after the steam whistle first blew. It was a red lens-lantern hung on a post about three hundred feet from the signal building, and was lit November 26, 1900. Two years later, the old fog-signal building was torn down and a new one built.

As vessel traffic increased and their routes moved farther from the coastline, aids at Point Montara were upgraded. In 1912 a fourth-order Fresnel lens was installed in a wood skeleton tower, and in 1919 the light in the lens was changed from incandescent oil vapor to incandescent electric. It could then be seen fourteen miles at sea. The old boilers and steam whistles were replaced by gas engines and diaphone signals.

In 1920 Walter White arrived with his wife, and three children. White came from Point Arguello and had earlier helped rebuild Point Arena after the 1906 earthquake. At Point Montara he was assistant keeper, and the family lived upstairs in the Victorian dwelling. Soon after they arrived, their fourth child, Laverne was born.

Laverne recalled that living upstairs was not easy for a family with four young children. "We had to be quiet," she said. Keepers needed their sleep during the day. "We talked in whispers. There was no slamming of doors." If the children were noisy, White heard about it from Keeper Dempsey who lived downstairs. In turn, "We caught it," said Laverne.

While at Point Montara, Laverne's mother, sister, and one brother contracted diptheria. Laverne was six at the time. To protect her from the disease she was sent to live with relatives in San Francisco. Her mother and sister recovered, but her brother died. Following the tragedy, Laverne's mother asked to leave Point Montara. The Lighthouse Bureau responded. White was promoted to principal keeper at Point Hueneme, and the family moved in 1927. A year following their departure, the present cast iron, thirty-foot high tower was built to hold the Fresnel lens.

Ed Wardell, docent at the Treasure Island Museum in San Francisco Bay, learned about Point Montara from his mother, Mary Elizabeth, who was born there. Wardell's grandfather, Nils Hall, was principal keeper from 1898 to 1912. The Hall's staples arrived by tender. Flour, rice, and sugar came in large cloth sacks, and when the sacks were empty, Wardell's grandmother washed them and used the material to make clothes for the

TED NELSON

The fog-signal building behind Point Montara's tower accommodates American Youth Hostel overnight guests.

83

five children. "For years my mother thought C & H Sugar made little girl's underclothes," said Wardell.

When the Halls left, Dempsey was promoted from assistant to principal keeper. In the 1930s Dempsey was still keeper, and Mary Elizabeth brought her family, including Wardell, who was then a young boy, to visit the station. "Back in those days you didn't visit empty handed," said Wardell. His father brought two bottles of homemade wine, and Mary Elizabeth brought a roast. "The Dempseys would put the roast away," said Wardell, and send the boys to collect a "trash dinner." With bucket in hand they gathered abalone, clams, and mussels.

After the Coast Guard assumed lighthouse management, Dempsey continued as keeper during the first years of World War II. At this time Point Montara was active with military units including a K9 Corps with men and dogs who patrolled the beaches. A coast artillery mobile unit was also stationed here.

Returned to its peace time status, the station was tended by three coast guardsmen until it was automated in 1970. Now an off-shore horn buoy has replaced the fog signal, and a small modern lens shines from the tower. The Fresnel lens is on exhibit at the San Mateo County Historical Society Museum.

Today, the station is part of the Golden Gate National Recreation Area. American Youth Hostels, Incorporated, provide overnight stays in the duplex built in 1961 and the 1902 fog-signal building.

Directions and Hours: Less than one-half mile south of Montara (town) watch for small AYH sign and turn west onto a dirt driveway. The hostel is closed from 9:30 A.M. to 4:30 P.M. Day use is available by prior arrangement for a charge. Phone (415) 728-7177.

Chapter 20

Point Bonita Lighthouse

The Point Bonita Lighthouse, anchored to a narrow ledge 124 feet above the sea, is four miles west of the Golden Gate Bridge. This is the second lighthouse built on the point. Its large lens, still flashing, and lantern are the originals used on the first tower established in 1855.

To reach the lighthouse visitors walk down a paved path below a radar tower where the first lighthouse once stood, pass a windy gap, and through a tunnel. Keepers walked this same route for over one hundred years. At the path's end a suspension bridge crosses a chasm to the lighthouse.

In the early 1850s, while other lighthouses were being built under the contract with the firm of Gibbons and Kelly, mariners were demanding that a lighthouse be built at Point Bonita.

Strong currents, rocks, shoals, and fog at this northwest entrance to the Golden Gate created hazardous sailing conditions. In 1853 the steamship *Tennesse* ploughed ashore north of Point Bonita at today's Tennesse Cove. In 1854 the clipper ship *San Francisco* sailing in fog struck the rocks at Point Bonita and sank east of the point in Bonita Cove.

Point Bonita's first lighthouse, a fifty-six foot brick tower stood 306 feet above the sea. On April 30, 1855, keeper Colsen lit the lamp in the second-order Fresnel lens.

The keepers' dwelling, Cape Cod style without the tower, was a short distance away. Quarters for two keepers were separated by stairs leading to an attic. This dwelling once stood near where today's paved path begins. Covered cisterns are still there.

In August 1856 California's first fog signal was installed at the point. It was a twenty-four pounder cannon fired by retired Sergeant Edward Maloney. During one foggy spell, Maloney fired the gun every half hour for three days and three nights with only two hours rest. The keepers would not relieve him. "I was nearly used up," he wrote. "All the rest I would require in twenty-four hours is two, if only I could get it." He soon resigned. Maloney's cannon is now at the Alameda Coast Guard Station.

Two years later the cannon was replaced briefly by a bell-boat anchored near the bar. Then a 1,500 pound fog bell hanging from a frame building near the tower's base clanged warnings.

Point Bonita, like Point Loma's first lighthouse, was plagued with fog. The tower and bell often were shrouded in fog while lower elevations were fog-free. During the 1870s the fog signal and lighthouse were reestablished on the precipitous ridges below.

Workers built a landing platform in Bonita Cove, and an incline railway, derrick, and tramway to lift building materials, and later supplies. They first built a fog-signal building in 1872. It was undermined by a landslide, and a second one was built. The tunnel, 118-feet long and still used today, was dug through solid rock in 1876. Two dwellings were built next to the original dwelling. The new lighthouse was built using the lantern and lens from the old tower, which was capped and used as a day mark.

On February 1, 1877, Keeper Captain John Briercliff Brown, lit the lamp. Brown had arrived at Point Bonita in 1872. He was happy with the new lighthouse. "I've stood my watch outside (the old tower) in the storm," he said, "rather than be inside when the walls was rockin' like the cradle in the deep." The new lighthouse, "...is steadier...and you can see the light a great deal better, so the ship masters say." Four men now tended the light and the two first-class steam sirens.

When Brown retired after twenty-seven years at Point Bonita, ship's owners and merchants honored the faithful keeper, and presented him with a gold-headed cane. They also noted that since 1872, Brown and his assistants, "...have dragged forty men from the sea under the light."

In 1901 Hermann and Freda Engel moved into the musty rooms of the Cape Cod dwelling. By then surfmen lived at the Point Bonita Life-Saving Station above the cove.

TED NELSON

Visitors cross a suspension bridge to reach the Point Bonita Lighthouse.

A year later, the present fog-signal building was built seaward of the lighthouse. The old Cape Cod dwelling needed replacement but little was done. It took the 1906 San Francisco earthquake to bring change.

The first shock at the station occurred on April 18 at 5:12 a.m. As told by their daughter, Norma Engel, in *Three Beams of Light*, Freda grabbed their two young sons, born since the Engel's arrival at the point, and rushed outside before the dwelling collapsed. No lives were lost. For the next two years, until new quarters were built, the Engels lived in an army engineer's office. The other keeper lived in the old fog-signal building. The original tower survived the earthquake but was torn down in 1907.

By 1915 a new dwelling stood on the site of the old fog-signal building. Foundation remnants can be seen at the east end of the suspension bridge. Assistant keeper Alex Martin lived there with his wife and young children. Though the yard was fenced, the children were tethered when playing outside in case they dropped off the cliff. One day Mrs. Martin saw the tether, but no daughter. She was dangling from its end down the cliff's side. The Martins later moved up the hill.

Until 1941 a narrow landbridge connected the lighthouse to the mainland. Then a landslide carried it away creating the chasm. The Coast Guard, then in charge of the station, built a wooden bridge and the suspension bridge in 1954.

By then, coast guardsmen and their families were living in comfortable homes near the lifeboat station that was later discontinued. They carried on the work of earlier keepers and monitored vessel traffic from a World War II watch shack built on the lighthouse.

Point Bonita was the last California lighthouse station to be automated. Its light and fog signal were switched to automatic in April 1981. Coast guardsman, Roger Hudspith, reluctant to leave the station, said the automatic fog signal, "...can't answer the phone or mow the lawn."

The lighthouse, painted, restored, and watch shack removed, was then turned over to the National Park Service. Coast Guard Group San Francisco, however, still maintains the light and fog signal.

Directions and Hours: The lighthouse is located in the Marin Headlands of the Golden Gate National Recreation Area. Access to the lighthouse is during guided walks on Saturday and Sunday afternoons and sunset tours every first and third Wednesdays. Phone: (415) 331-1540.

Chapter 21

Point Reyes Lighthouse

Point Reyes is one of the foggiest and windiest points on the west coast. It was and is remote. To reach the lighthouse visitors drive across open uplands and through large cattle ranches that date back to the 1850s.

Vessels approaching from the north turned at the point on their way to the Golden Gate, and mariners pressed the Lighthouse Service to build a light and fog signal here. In 1854 money was appropriated, but clouded land titles and owners asking extravagant prices delayed construction. In 1860 an angered California senator told the Senate, "...The commerce between California and Oregon is suffering constantly for want of a lighthouse."

In 1861 with no signals to guide him, the captain of the clipper ship *Sea Nymph* became confused by fog-shrouded land marks. Thinking he was entering the Golden Gate and with all sails set, he ploughed into Point Reyes Beach. Six more ships were wrecked at Point Reyes before a deed for eighty-three acres was signed in 1869.

According to Dewey Livingston in *The History and Architecture of the Point Reyes Light Station,* the original lighthouse plans called for a Cape Cod style dwelling with tower, located at the top of the point. Officials, however, decided high fog would obscure the light and relocated the site 275 feet down the bluff where the tower stands today.

Materials were landed at Drakes Bay and hauled by oxcart to the top of the point. A two-story duplex was built where today's Park Service apartments stand. A retaining wall, thirteen feet high in one place, was built

89

TED NELSON

Over 300 steps lead down to the Point Reyes Lighthouse.

around the dwelling and backfilled with soil to create a garden spot for the keepers. John C. Bull, principal keeper, and his wife, who was his assistant, were the first to move in.

Meanwhile, Joseph Bien started building the thirty-seven foot tall tower. It, like Cape Mendocino which Bien built earlier, was constructed with forged iron plates bolted into concrete. He also installed the imported lighting apparatus. For his work, Bien requested and was paid by the tower's weight, eighteen cents a pound. On December 1, 1870, Bull lit the lamp in the rotating, first-order Fresnel lens. It stood 294 feet above the water.

Before construction began on the fog signal, the contractor lowered himself on a rope about one hundred feet below the lighthouse and selected a site. Rock was blasted, and, "An iron railing was put around the edges of the plot prepared for the signal to keep anyone from rolling off into the sea..." By June 1871 a twelve-inch steam whistle was ready to operate, but remained silent until winter rains filled the cisterns. This was only the beginning of problems.

A year later the fog-signal building burned, and when rebuilt, the signal again lacked sufficient water to operate. The cistern and rain catchment basin were enlarged. One year a local rancher hauled twenty thousand gallons of water to fill the cisterns.

When the fog signal worked, it blew and blew. In 1887 keepers shoveled one hundred tons of coal to operate the signal 2070 hours. After the signal had blown seven days and nights without ceasing, a *San Francisco Chronicle* reporter wrote, "...the jaded attendants looked as if they had been on a protracted spree." Coal was stored in sacks in a building just above the lighthouse. From there the sacks slid down a chute to the signal.

Point Reyes was seldom an assignment of choice for the four keepers who tended the station. In addition to fog and wind, there were the stairs. In the early days there were six hundred steps to the lighthouse, and three hundred more down to the fog signal. The Chronicle reporter continued, "When the storms are their worst, spray dashes up two hundred feet..." The keepers' "...only safety is in crawling on hands and knees up and down...the stairs."

The isolation bothered some keepers. The nearest town was twenty miles over rough wagon roads. One assistant keeper found solace in drink. When his whiskey bottle was empty, he consumed the alcohol used for cleaning station lamps. Other keepers attended local dances or functions held at nearby ranches.

Keepers usually didn't stay long at Point Reyes except Paulus Nillson. He was a first assistant in 1897, and became principal keeper in 1909. On

February 18, 1921, the log reported that Nillson fell and was badly injured. He died three days later. He and his wife had lived at the Point Reyes station for twenty-four years.

The Lighthouse Service continued to upgrade the fog signal, and in 1915 installed a diaphone signal powered by gasoline engines. Mariners "applauded" this effective signal. In 1934 the fog signal was relocated just below the lighthouse, and four years later the light and fog signal began operating electrically.

Even with the navigation aids shipwrecks occurred. A local story tells that San Francisco newspapers always had headline type ready, "Ship Aground at Point Reyes." In 1927 gale force winds smashed a fishing boat into the rocks at Point Reyes. For hours three desperate, wet fishermen clung to the rocks below the lighthouse until keeper Fred Kreth climbed down the rugged cliff. He dropped the men a rope and assisted each one to safety.

After the Coast Guard took over in 1939, more changes were made, roads were improved and concrete steps built. Despite the fog and wind, visitors came to see the lighthouse and the California murre, which nested on the point's rocks. There were so many visitors that escorting them said one of the Coast Guard keepers, "...has become a major portion of the duties of men assigned."

In the 1960 the Coast Guard razed the 1885 keepers' cottages, a 1901 weather bureau building, and the original dwelling. A four-unit apartment was built on the site of the old dwelling. Cisterns and a watershed remain and can be seen when visiting the station.

In 1975 the station was automated, and a small building was built to hold an automated flashing light, foghorn, and radio beacon. The tower and original Fresnel lens were left intact. Two years later the station was transferred to the Point Reyes National Seashore who maintain the lighthouse and open it for tours and occasional evening lightings.

Directions and Hours: Point Reyes Lighthouse, is located about twenty miles west of Highway 1. Follow National Park signs from the highway between Olema and Point Reyes Station. Hours are from 10 A.M. to 5 P.M. Thursday through Monday. The stairs close at 4:30 P.M. Access inside the tower is by guided tour. Phone: (415) 669-1534.

Chapter 22

Farallon Islands Lighthouse

The Farallon Islands are a group of islets standing about twenty-three miles west of San Francisco Bay. Southeast Farallon Island is the largest. This rugged islet, pyramidal in shape and 350 feet high was selected as the site for California's third lighthouse. Its construction was under the contract with Gibbons and Kelly.

In early 1853 the contractor's bark *Oriole* came to Southeast Farallon Island with supplies and workmen to build the lighthouse. Contruction work at Alcatraz and Fort Point was proceeding nicely. Things would be different on the Farallons, however, as told by Peter White in *The Keeper's Log*.

First there was a problem with the "egg pickers." The islands were the nesting sites of over 400,000 common murres. This seabird colony produced "...rich, delicate, and altogether desireable..." eggs. At $1.50 per dozen in the San Francisco market the egg business was lucrative. The Pacific Egg Company which controlled the trade at the time did not want intruders. An uneasy truce was developed to allow construction to begin.

Like other early California lighthouses, the Farallon Islands station was to be a one and one-half story keeper's dwelling with the light tower extending through the center of the gabled roof. It was soon discovered that this design was unworkable here. The contractors wrote, "The only spot where a light can be placed...is...on the summit of a percipitous mass of rock...the summit is so narrow that it is impossible to obtain a base for a dwelling house..."

93

It was decided to build the tower at the summit and the keeper's dwelling on a more level spot below. Major Hartman Bache, experienced in lighthouse construction, was placed in charge.

The construction environment was even more unfriendly than the "egg pickers." White stated, "...there was no suitable anchorage at the island ...and the completion of a dock was out of the question..." A hoist was set up for "...snatching cargoes from a small boat..." Once landed, the material had to be carried by hand up the steep slopes. Bache is quoted as saying, "...the bricks (must be) transported on men's backs by fours and fives...the operation is second to impossible."

Still, by November 1853 the dwelling was completed, and the tower stood ready to receive its lens. The first-order Fresnel did not arrive from France until December 1854. Bache had the seventy-three crates containing the lens' parts sent to the island. As assembly began, it became apparent that this light too was plagued with the same problem encounterd by some other early California lighthouses. The lens was too big for the squat brick tower on the island's peak.

Exasperated, Bache tore the first tower down. Over the protests of his superiors he purchased a mule to help haul supplies and started to build another. Almost a year later, in December 1855, the Farallon light was in operation.

White described the difficulties faced by the Lighthouse Service in hiring keepers. Gold rush economics prevailed, and the station, as described later by Charles Nordhoff was, "...so wholly desolate, so entirely separated from the world," that Congress had to raise the wages for Farallon keepers to entice them to the island.

The struggle over the egg business later erupted into armed violence between rival "egger" groups. Two men were killed in what had become known as the Egg War. In 1881 egg collecting was made illegal, but into the early 1900s small ships made clandestine trips to the island during the egg season.

In 1858, the ship *Lucas* foundered on the island in the fog. Twenty-three people were lost. The ingenious Bache then devised a fog signal. It was a train whistle described by the *Coast Pilot* as "...erected over a natural hole ...connected with and open to the ocean, and as blown by the rush of air through the passage, caused by the sea breaking into its mouth."

In the early 1880s a new first-class, steam siren was put into place. This project, too, would have tried Bache's patience. The excavations for the signal's cisterns opened veins of mineral water containing enough free sulphuric acid to slack the cistern's mortar. All the brick work had to be redone.

With the new fog signal came the construction of two Victorian duplexes. This allowed all the keepers to have their families on the remote island. By 1897 the orignal keeper's dwelling was being used as a schoolhouse.

In 1905, the navy established an "experimental wireless telegraph" station on the island. Maxine Smith lived on the island with her husband during World War II. She recalled hearing that the station was an important communication link during the 1906 San Francisco earthquake and later, the first west coast station to achieve wireless contact with the Hawaiian Islands. She also remembered the island grave of "Paddy" the mule, a later successor to Major Bache's mule.

The lighthouse station was automated in 1972, and a rotating aero beacon now turns atop the base of Bache's second tower. The Victorian duplexes still stand. The island is within the Point Reyes Farallon Islands National Marine Sanctuary. Resident scientists study one of the world's richest marine ecosystems, including the murres, whose eggs are now safe from the "egg pickers."

Directions and Hours: The original first-order lens can be seen at the Treasure Island Maritime Museum. Daily hours are 10 A.M. to 3:30 P.M. The museum is closed Thanksgiving, Christmas, New Years, and Easter. Phone: (415) 395-5067. Though the Farallon Islands are off limits, all day tours arc scheduled by Oceanic Society Expeditions to the waters around the islets. They operate June through November. Phone: (415) 441-1106.

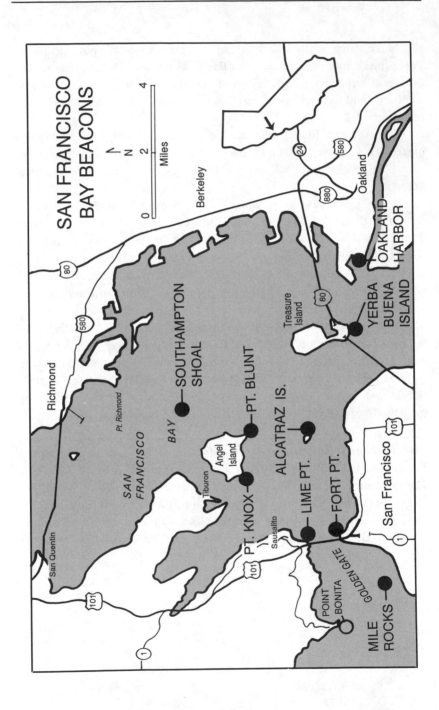

Section 6

San Francisco Bay Beacons

In 1769 Spanish soldiers traveling overland up California's coast under the command of Gaspar de Portola, became the first recorded Europeans to see San Francisco Bay. Six years later Juan Manuel de Alaya, with the ship's launch leading the way, brought the *San Carlos* into the bay. Thus the *San Carlos* became the first ship to sail through the Golden Gate, a name applied later by the explorer John Charles Fremont.

In 1869, one hundred years after the soldiers first saw the bay, over six hundred ships entered the Golden Gate. The transcontinental railroad was being completed and wealth was flowing from California's gold fields, Nevada's silver mines and the rich farms of the Central Valley.

In that year the *Coast Pilot* called the bay, "...emphatically the port of the Pacific (with) its noble entrance and bold shores, the Sacramento and its tributaries draining the rich agricultural valleys and auriferous slopes of the Sierra Nevada, the magic city upon its shores."

In addition to the ships entering the bay in 1869, hundreds of other vessels were plying its waters. Scows delivered hay, tugs assisted sailing ships, ferries carried passangers, and steamboats made regular runs to Central Valley river ports.

Mariners were already being assisted by lighthouses on Alcatraz Island and at Fort Point. Later, more stations were added, some beginning only as fog signals. They included stations on Lime Point, Angel Island, Mile Rocks, Oakland Harbor, Southampton Shoal, and Yerba Buena Island, the site of a lighthouse depot.

COAST GUARD MUSEUM NORTHWEST

Alcatraz Island's second lighthouse. It replaced California's first lighthouse and was near the scene of prison riots.

Chapter 23

Alcatraz Island Lighthouse

The Alcatraz Island Lighthouse was the first U.S. lighthouse on the Pacific Coast. On June 1, 1854, from its island location in San Francisco Bay, the light shone out through the Golden Gate, across empty hills to the north and east, and over hundreds of ships lying abandoned off San Francisco, their crews long gone to the gold fields.

A few surviving log entries hint at the history witnessed by the Alcatraz keepers from their vantage point in the bay. April 18, 1906, "5:30 A.M. violent and continuous earthquake—San Francisco on fire..." March 8, 1945, "At 1030 today the Heroes of Battan arrived home on a troopship and were given a heroes welcome." May 1, 1946, "The Aircraft Carrier Saratoga left for the Bikini Atolls at 11:00 hrs."

The name Alcatraz has been synonymous with the prison since the federal penitentiary was established on the island in 1934. But the island's name has a more benign beginning. The word alcatraces means pelican in Spanish. It was given to today's Yerba Buena Island by the Spaniard Ayala, as he explored the bay in 1775. Later, the name was transfered to the island in the middle of the bay, and in 1851 the U.S. Coast Survey shortened the name to Alcatraz.

The Coast Survey was the bureau charged with selecting the sites for the west coast's first lighthouses, and by 1851 the initial site selections had been made. Thus, began the saga of the bark *Oriole* and California's first lighthouses.

In April 1852 the government contracted with Francis A. Gibbons and Francis X. Kelly to construct seven lighthouses in California and one in Washington Territory. Alcatraz Island was one of the sites selected.

The contractors dispatched the bark *Oriole* around Cape Horn from Baltimore, Maryland, laden with workmen and all the necessary building supplies except the materials for the external walls, which were to be obtained locally.

The *Oriole* arrived at San Francisco on January 29, 1853. An advanced party of workmen had come by way of the Isthmus of Panama, and when the ship arrived, they had already laid the foundation of the Alcatraz Island Lighthouse. By July 1853 the one and one-half story Cape Cod style lighthouse was complete. A short tower with a lantern on top rose through the center of the small building, but there was no lens.

The Alcatraz Lighthouse, along with the other seven lighthouses, had been designed to use Argand lamps and parobolic reflectors, an ineffective system that the old U.S. Lighthouse Establishment had clung stubbornly to. But, in 1852 the newly created Lighthouse Board adopted French-made Fresnel lenses for use in all major U.S. lighthouses.

A change order was issued to the contractors, and Lieutenant Washington A. Bartlett was sent to France to secure the necessary lenses. In October 1853 Alcatraz's fixed, third-order Fresnel lens was delivered to San Francisco, but the Treasury Department had no funds for its installation. Another eight months passed before the light was lit by the first keeper, Michael Cassin.

In 1856 a fog-signal bell was installed on the island's south side. The keepers had tended the station in isolation for only a short time when the Army begin to occupy the island. The lighthouse soon overlooked gun emplacements.

In 1883 a new fog bell "...weighing 3,340 pounds was cast at Mare Island Navy-Yard from the old bell and other material..." A new structure was built to house the bell. A year later mineral oil lamps replaced the lard oil lamps in the tower, and in 1900 a second fog-signal bell was added on the island's north shore.

In 1902, the original lens was crated up and sent to the lighthouse at Cape St. Elias in Alaska. It was replaced by a fourth-order Fresnel lens with its light flashing white every fifteen seconds.

B. F. Leeds was a long time head keeper on the island. His terse log entries describe both the mundane and the tragic. February 1, 1890, "Henry Hanson dismissed from the L.B. Service for drunkiness." September 14, 1890, "Hauled up dirt and manure for the flower garden." January 29, 1891, "Dr. Dietz killed his wife and himself, he was insane." A few days later Leeds wrote that, "Capt. Tyler left with little Wallace Dietz for N.Y."

At the age of seventy, Leeds was still serving when the 1906 San Francisco earthquake occurred. He wrote, "... is this the end of the world?...Terrible seeing S.F. from here."

In 1909 expansion of the military prison then on the island overshadowed the original lighthouse. It was replaced by an imposing tower built of reinforced concrete with connecting quarters for three keepers. The eighty-four foot tower near the island's summit placed the focal plane of the lens 214 feet above the bay. The new station used an electric arc light in the tower, and electricity operated fog sirens on the north and south sides of the island.

With the prison came events not normally associated with a light keeper's "lonely vigil." The log for early May 1946 carries a special page. "1430 hrs convict on the loose with a submachine gun, entire prison held at bay, shooting is almost continuous...U.S. Marines landed on north end of island...fire again raging in the cell blocks...hand grenades being dropped through holes broken through the roof." After nearly two days the riot was finally quelled. The keeper wrote, "The end of 44 hours of HELL."

Alcatraz was one of the first lighthouses to be automated. On November 22, 1963, the Coast Guard reported that, "From now on the (lighthouse) will be operated by remote control from the Coast Guard station near Fort Point."

In 1969, after closure of the penitentiary, a group of Native Americans occupied the island for over a year. They claimed the surplus government property as theirs under an 1868 Sioux Treaty. During this period, many of the structures were vandalized, and the keepers' quarters were burned.

Today, the 1909 tower still stands displaying a modern, white flashing optic. The fourth-order Fresnel lens can be seen at the island's museum.

Directions and Hours: The island is a part of Golden Gate National Recreation Area. Tours are available from pier 41 near Fisherman's Wharf. Advanced reservations are recommended. Phone: (415) 546-2896.

TED NELSON

Fort Point's third light tower stands on a parapet beneath the Golden Gate Bridge.

Chapter 24

Fort Point Lighthouse

The last vestige of California's second built lighthouse station is a small, steel tower perched on the upper parapet of Fort Point. The tower is dwarfed by the fort and the steel girders of the Golden Gate Bridge that arch above. The little tower, with its lamp and lens long removed, was the third lighthouse built on the point.

Fort Point's first lighthouse was built under the contract with Francis A. Gibbons and Francis X. Kelly. Workmen and supplies arrived from Baltimore aboard the bark *Oriole*.

Construction of the lighthouse began concurrently with the work on the Alcatraz Island Lighthouse. The twenty-eight by thirty-foot Cape Cod style structure, identical to the one on Alcatraz Island, was finished in 1853 shortly after Alcatraz's completion. It thus became California's second lighthouse. Waiting for its third-order Fresnel lens to arrive from France, the lighthouse stood empty on the low point at the south side of the Golden Gate.

In the year the lighthouse was completed, Congress agreed with a board of military engineers that the point should serve the army in the bay's defense. Funds were authorized for a major fort on the point, and the new lighthouse was torn down to make way for it. Its third-order lens was never installed at Fort Point. Instead, it was sent to Point Piños Lighthouse on Monterey Bay, where the lens has remained for 138 years.

Construction of the large fortress began in 1854, and seven years later the three-story brick fort was completed.

A light was still needed at the point. While men worked on the fort, a truncated, wooden tower, thirty-six feet high was built between the fort and its seawall. Its light was shown from a fifth-order lens in March 1855. This was California's third operating light behind Alcatraz Island and Point Piños.

The seawall proved inadequate against the Golden Gate's currents and storm waves rolling in from the Pacific. Again the point's lighthouse had to be torn down, this time to make way for rebuilding the seawall with granite blocks.

Fort Point's third lighthouse in eleven years was built in 1864. This time a twenty-seven foot high, iron tower stood atop the fort at its northwest bastion. It was designed so that in the event of war it could be dismantled quickly. An open, circular stairway led to a small watch room where stairs continued up to the lantern room which housed a fifth-order lens. The lens was turned by a clockwork drive that required winding every two and one-half hours.

A fog bell was added. It hung in a housing cantilevered from the fort's side. To maintain the bell's mechanism, or to strike the bell by hand in the event of mechanical failure, the station's keepers had to climb down a precarious ladder that passed in front of a gun port. In 1880 a larger bell, formerly used as an auxillary at Yerba Buena Island replaced the point's first bell. The Lighthouse Board reported that this bell, "...now answers all the requirements of a fog signal at this station."

But in 1899, the Board proposed that the bell be replaced by a Daboll trumpet, saying that the bell was,"... inadequate both in position and power." To William Ward, Captain of the *City of Rio de Janeiro*, these were prophetic words.

Early on the morning of February 22, 1901, the Pacific Mail Steamship Company's *Rio*, inbound from Hong Kong, was working its way into San Francisco Bay. Capt. Ward and a pilot were in the wheelhouse. Below, 227 passengers and crew members were readying for their arrival in San Francisco. Approaching Fort Point, the ship entered a wall of fog. A lookout was sent forward in the darkness. At 5:25 a.m. the ship ploughed onto a rocky ledge, its bow thrust upward.

The *Rio* settled back and seemed to lodge on the reef. Capt. Ward lashed the ship's horn halyard to the wheel to keep it blaring and began to direct an orderly evacuation by the lifeboats. Suddenly, without warning the ship slid off the rocks and began sinking. Despite the horn's mournful blast, none of the sleeping soldiers at the fort nor the nearby life-saving station were alerted to the ship's plight.

The quickness of the sinking and an inadequate number of lifeboats resulted in the loss of 140 lives. It was to be the bay's worst sea disaster. As the ship went down, Capt. Ward returned to his cabin to perish with his ship.

The 1901 Lighthouse Board report stated, "The recent disaster to the steamer *Rio de Janeiro* on the reef…might not have occurred if an efficient signal had been in operation here." But, not until 1904 was the recommended compressed air Daboll trumpet installed on the fort's bastion near the tower. Two years before, the old lens had been replaced with a fourth-order revolving lens that flashed alternately red and white.

Two keeper's dwellings stood on a bluff above the fort. The early keepers had to descend the bluff and cross a windy gap between the fort and the bluff to reach the light. The Lighthouse Board called it, "…a very dangerous task on dark and stormy nights." In 1876 a bridge was built from the bluff to the fort's top.

Two years later, James Rankin became principal keeper at Fort Point. His wife, Nellie, quoted in *The Fort Point Salvo*, recalling their new home said, "I had to climb 250 steps…Oh my!" When tenders arrived, all of their supplies were carried up the steps until a tramway was built in 1898.

Rankin retired after forty-one years at the station. During his career here, he had rescued eighteen people from drowning. The last two rescues were made just months before his retirement when, at age seventy-five, he twice leaped the seawall to save drowning boys.

The Golden Gate Bridge was completed in 1937. In 1952 Coast guardsman S.J. Bodilsen wrote, "During the construction of the Golden Gate Bridge, (which made the light superflous,) it became my job to discontinue this station—to remove the fog-signal equipment and to remove the lens from the lantern on the tower. It always makes me sad to see a lighthouse go out of business."

Directions and Hours: The Fort Point National Historic Site is reached by turning off Lincoln Boulevard at Long Avenue. The fort is open from 10 A.M. to 5 P.M. daily except Christmas, Thanksgiving, and New Years. Phone: (415) 556-1693.

TED NELSON

Only Lime Point's fog-signal building remains near the north tower of the Golden Gate Bridge.

Chapter 25

Lime Point Lighthouse

All that remains of the 1883 Lime Point light station is the original fog-signal building. Seen from Fort Point the building appears as a white speck near the massive north tower of the Golden Gate Bridge. The Lime Point headland rises steeply to the west, the Marin hills roll behind.

The station is on a low, rocky spur that juts from the headland at the Golden Gates's narrowest point. Its initial purpose, as a fog signal, was to protect mariners in the dense fog that regularly rolls through the Gate from the Pacific. A small lens lantern was added later. When the fog signal went into operation on September 10, 1883, Lime Point had all the elements of a major station, except there was neither a tower nor a light. A large fog-signal building was located at the end of the rocky spur housing duplicate coal-fired boilers and engines to power the two steam whistles. From a coal shed the keepers shoveled 250 pounds of coal per hour when the fog-signal was in operation.

A two-story keepers' dwelling, with room for two keepers and their families, stood behind the fog-signal building. A third story was added later and the brick, white painted buildings gave the appearance of a Mediterranean villa on the shore of the bay.

A 20,000 gallon water tank was connected by a pipe line to a spring near Lime Point Cove. In the station's early years, however, there was either too much rain or not enough spring water. In the first autumn of operation, a second spring was tapped to furnish an adequate supply of water; the previous winter heavy rains had caused a landslide that damaged the new water tank. More tanks were built to increase the station's water storage capacity for the summer months, while the trail to Sausalito had to be cleared of mud slides almost every winter.

In 1900 a white, lens lantern was established at the station and a small oil house was built. Two years later, the Lighthouse Service began to experiment with oil as an alternative to coal in the station's fog-signal boilers.

The results were gratifying. The oil resulted in an intense flame without smoke and reduced costs. When the fog signal operated for a full day, coal for the boilers had cost $25.44. With oil at seventy-five cents per forty-two gallon barrel, the cost of twenty-four hours of operation fell to $6.91. The boilers were converted to oil, and the keepers no longer had to satisfy the boiler's prodigious appetite for coal with their shovels.

In 1923 a secondary light and electric siren were established at Point Diablo, near Bonita Cove. They were maintained by the Lime Point keepers.

On the evening of June 3, 1960, the station's fog signal, then converted to compressed air, was in operation. Coast guardsman Nieves Saldate was clearing his dinner dishes when he witnessed an event rare in the annals of fog-signal stations. The 440-foot freighter *India Bear* sailed directly into the station. Saldate said, "It made plenty of noise and shook the house...I ran out and there she was, right in front of my face."
The ship's prow was badly dented. A newspaper account said the ship had, "...sliced seven feet into a solid concrete causeway and demolished the light station's outdoor toilet."

The station was automated in 1961 and the residence was later removed. The original fog-signal building, now behind a fence, can be seen with a short walk from the end of Fort Baker road leading south from Sausalito. The point provides an unexcelled view of the bay and San Francisco beyond.

Chapter 26

Angel Island's Lighthouses

Angel Island is the largest island in San Francisco Bay. Shaped like a battered, three-cornered hat, it is tucked into the bay's northwest end. Sausalito lies west of the island. The Tiburon Peninsula lies to the north across Racoon Strait.

Miwok Indians greeted Ayala when he anchored in a cove on the island's north side in 1775. From there the Spanish explorer went on to produce the first chart of the bay. Through its history, the island was a Mexican cattle ranch, a quarantine and immigration station, a point for processing World War II prisoners, and a U.S. missile base.

A fog-signal station using a bell was established on Point Knox at the island's southwest corner in 1886. John Ross was the first keeper. He retired in 1902. The station's log noted that he had, "...faithfully tended the bell, accompanied by his wife and two children." Responsibilty for the station then fell upon Mrs. Juliet Fish Nichols. Her faithfulness to the keeper's duties would become legendary.

Juliet was born in China in 1859. Her mother died at childbirth, and Juliet's aunt, Emily, married Juliet's father, Dr. Melancthon Fish. Dr. Fish brought his family to Oakland after service in the Civil War. There, Juliet married Commander Henry Nichols. The marriage would lead Juliet and her stepmother to careers as lighthouse keepers.

Their story is told by Clifford Gallant in *The Keeper's Log*. Commander Nichols had served in the Coast and Geodetic Survey before becoming District Inspector for California's lighthouses in 1892. In that role, he helped Emily Fish become keeper at Point Piños. Nichols, later promoted to Captain, died in the Philippines during the Spanish-American War. His widow was appointed keeper at the Angel Island station in 1902.

Juliet came to the station by government steamer, crossed a military reservation, and then climbed down 151 steps to reach the one-story residence. In front of the dwelling, a fog bell hung in a small house perched precariously over the point. Also, there was a lens lantern that had been added in 1901.

It was the bell's faulty mechanism that lead to the legend of Juliet's devotion as a keeper. Her log book for early July 1906 stated, "Bell struck by hand 20 hrs. 35 mts." Gallant's account is more vivid. It stated that Juliet watched the fog roll through the Golden Gate and heard other fog horns begin their mournful sounds. She started her fog bell mechanism. "A few minutes later it broke down, and there was no time for repairs since she could see through the fog the masts of a sailing vessel aproaching. She grabbed a hammer and frantically pounded the bell." The vessel veered away. With the immediate danger passed, "...Juliet rang the bell in its proscribed manner." After more than twenty hours, "...the fog lifted and she was able to rest."

Juliet's experience underscored the importance of fog signals on the bay. After the Point Knox signal began operation, the Lighthouse Board began recommending that a fog bell be placed on Quarry Point on the island's east side. The Board noted that more vessels passed between the island and Southampton Shoal than anywhere else in California, except for the Golden Gate. They were bound, "...to and from the great grain wharves at Port Costa (on Carquinez Strait), and the Sacramento and San Joaquin rivers..."

It wasn't until 1915, a year after Juliet Nichols' retirement, that additional signals were placed on the island. Fog bells and lens lanterns were established on Point Blunt on the island's southeast corner and on Point Stuart, a short distance north of Point Knox. These new stations were the responsibility of the one keeper at Point Knox.

In 1939 the original keepers dwelling was made into a two-story structure. But, in 1961 the demise of Juliet Nichols' station was signaled when the Coast Guard moved the island's center of operations to new facilities at Point Blunt.

The old keeper's dwelling at Point Knox was burned down in 1973. In 1976 the gradual process of automation led to the removal of all resident Coast Guard personnel on the island.

Today, Angel Island is a state park and can be reached by tour boat for hiking and bicycling. Little remains of the island's lighthouse history. Though not accessible, Juliet's bell still remains on a wooden platform at Point Knox.

Directions and Hours: For commercial tour boat access to the island call 1-800-BAY-CRUISE.

RALPH SHANKS, NAUTICAL RESEARCH CENTRE

The Point Knox station on Angel Island where Juliet Nichols rang the fog bell for twenty hours.

COAST GUARD MUSEUM NORTHWEST

Coastguardsmen land at Mile Rocks Lighthouse from a small boat.

Chapter 27

Mile Rocks Lighthouse

This lighthouse described as a "four-story steel wedding cake," was established in 1906. Though the upper part of the structure is gone, lights on its base still serve as a navigational aid marking the southern side of the channel into San Francisco Bay. This lonely, topless sentinel can be seen from vista points west of the Golden Gate Bridge.

Between the two large Mile Rocks and Land's End, other rocks often awash were described by the Lighthouse Board as, "...particularly dangerous because of the eddying currents and fogs that prevail in that vicinity."

In 1889 the Lighthouse Service anchored a bell-buoy near the rocks, but strong currents repeatedly plunged the buoy beneath the water, and it was removed. Other ideas were suggested including a fog signal. At the time, however, the larger rock's size, forty by thirty feet, was considered too small for a permanent structure.

In 1901 with the urgent plea of the San Francisco Chamber of Commerce influenced by the sinking of the *City of Rio de Janerio* several months earlier, the Board decided to build a lighthouse and fog signal at Mile Rocks.

It was not an easy task. The first crew seeing waves wash over Mile Rock quit. A second crew began work in September 1904. A small motor schooner fitted as quarters for the men was moored near the rock. During a heavy blow, it dragged its anchors and was then moved to a safer area. The men rode from the schooner to Mile Rock by launch. Often they were unable to land, and seldom could they work a full day. Some fell into the water but were rescued before currents carried them out to sea.

113

By June 1905 the thirty-four foot high concrete base was completed, covering the entire rock. Its walls, enclosed in steel, were four feet thick. Subsequently, three floors, each smaller than the lower one, were added and topped by the lantern room containing a third-order Fresnel lens. The light, showing fixed, red, was seventy-eight feet above the water. Both the light and fog signal began operating in the winter of 1906.

This was a four keeper station, and families lived on shore. Supplies and people boarded the lighthouse by two derricks, one on either side, each with a fifty-foot rope ladder suspended from the end. During calm seas, entry to the lighthouse was through a door in its base.

Despite difficulties getting aboard the lighthouse, visitors came. In 1915 thirteen-year-old, Gaynel Dresser, signed the visitors' book. Five years later, engaged to be married, she decided she wanted a wedding "with a kick in it," and chose the lighthouse for the ceremony.

On a foggy February day Gaynel, wearing heels, a fur hat and wool coat, climbed from a pitching boat and up the slippery rope ladder. Her fiance, the minister, and parents followed. While the keepers watched, the couple were married on the gallery outside the lantern.

This occasion provided novelty for the men whose life was often lonely and exasperating, especially, when the fog signal blew. The confined quarters offered no escape from the blast of the ten-inch whistle.

Mile Rocks was automated in 1965. The lantern room and top three stories were removed; a helicopter pad was built on the remaining structure. The Supertyphon air horns installed earlier were retained, and a rotating aero beacon was installed. The original Fresnel lens now beams from the Old Point Loma Lighthouse in San Diego.

Though automated, the lighthouse was difficult to maintain. Electric shore cables broke, and generators mal-functioned. The Coast Guard proposed down grading the light. The San Francisco Bay Pilot Association objected, and today, Mile Rocks is powered by the sun.

Chapter 28

Oakland Harbor and Southampton Shoal Lighthouses

The Oakland Harbor and Southampton Shoal lighthouses were added to the bay's retinue of light stations around the turn of the century. Each stood on piling in the bay's shallows. Their stories are entwined with the railroads that reached the bay's eastside.

In 1869, amid a thirty-seven gun salute, a Central Pacific train steamed into Oakland linking the Pacific Coast and the east by rail. Oakland lay along a salt water slough and an estuary that opened onto the bay. Some small wharfs had been built on the estuary, but now a major port was needed.

In the 1870s two piers, 750 feet apart and two miles long, were built into the bay beside the estuary and a channel was dredged. In 1879 the Lighthouse Board received an appropriation for a, "...small lighthouse and fog-bell..." at the end of the north pier. Land title problems and other delays prevented prompt construction, and it wasn't until January 27, 1890, that a fixed, white light shone from the fifth-order lens of the Oakland Harbor Lighthouse.

The station's design was reminiscent of California's first lighthouses. A short tower protruded through the center of a gable roof. A walkway surrounded the wooden building, which held a fog bell and a water tank. The approximately twenty by twenty-foot dwelling stood on eleven piles driven into the bay's mud. The structure was located west of the north pier which served as the railroad's wharf.

115

COAST GUARD MUSEUM NORTHWEST

The second Oakland Harbor Lighthouse after it was surrounded by the harbor's pier.

Assistant keeper, Hermann Engel, rowed his new wife, Freda, to the station in November 1900. Their daughter, Norma Engel, recounted that day in her book, *Three Beams of Light.* She described the gallant Irish keeper who welcomed them to their new home, and his willingness to make room for them. Freda inspected the little house. She saw that, "...the old wooden tub (in the station's outhouse) would have to be dragged into the kitchen when it came bath time." As she contemplated the eight by eight foot bedroom, "...a horrendous 'BONG" resounded through the room." The 3500-pound fog bell, ringing at five second intervals, was, "...just ten feet from the head of the bed."

The Engels also noted that the lighthouse shuddered with the bell's clang. The station's untreated piles had been attacked by marine borers, and though shored up with rock and the piles encased in concrete, the structure was unsound.

The Engels moved to Point Bonita in 1901. A year later, the Lighthouse Board concluded that a newlighthouse was needed. The old station was, "...liable to collapse at any time."

By July 11, 1903, a light shone from a new structure. This time the foundations were built to thwart marine borers. Piles, surrounded by concrete encased in steel cylinders, were driven to hard bottom. The building stood several feet above the water on steel beams with supporting concrete arches.

This second lighthouse was a grand affair compared to the first. In the white, two-story building the lower story contained the storerooms; the two keepers and their families lived above. An ornate railing swept around the balcony surrounding the second story. The balcony held the fog bell and a large water tank. At the top where the four-sided roofs converged, there was a short tower and lantern room.

The new lighthouse stood near the site of the old one, which had been dismantled, and as the port grew, the piers were extended, eventually reaching the station. The row boat was then little used, for the keepers and their families could drive to the lighthouse down the long pier, passing transcontinental trains, backed almost to the lighthouse door.

The lighthouse was discontinued in 1966 when an automatic beacon was placed in front of the old building. The lantern was removed and sent to Santa Cruz for use at the memorial lighthouse there. The building was sold to a restaurant firm and barged up the estuary.

As the Central Pacific had been to Oakland, the Santa Fe Railroad was to Richmond. In 1900 the Santa Fe began ferry service between Point Richmond and San Francisco. The southeast point of Southampton Shoal, with only three fathoms of water, lay on the ferry's course. A lighthouse was built on the shoal in 1905.

In December of that year, Samuel Hounsell became the station's first keeper. Two years later, he completed the long Lighthouse Service form titled "Description of Light Station." Regarding the light's characteristic Hounsell wrote, "Fixed white." Regarding a wharf or landing, the hand written entry stated, "No wharf, landing is made by means of a swinging ladder." Item by item the keeper described the three-story frame building with its winding stair from "basement" to tower landing.

The "Illuminating Apparatus" was described as a "Lens lantern with an arc of 360 degrees." The fog bell was noted as being made of bronze and weighing 3,500 pounds. The clockwork mechanism struck a double blow

Southampthon Shoal Lighthouse with its fog bell on the second balcony.

at five and fifteen second intervals and required winding every forty minutes.

The form's terse entries did not do justice to the the station. The white, three-story structure stood boldly over the shoal on eleven cylindrical piles. The tower and lantern room rose from the center of the four-sided roof. Balconies surrounded the first and second stories, and dormers were set back into the roof over the third story. The first, or basement, story was used for stores. Two keepers and their families occupied the rooms above. The station's boat hung on davits from the lower balcony, and the bell and large water tank stood on the balcony above.

The steel encased concrete cylinders were designed to stop marine borers. But, a new menace occurred shortly after the station's completion. The tidal current began eroding the sand around the cylinders, and rock was placed around the piles to further support them. In the 1906 earthquake, several of the piles were tilted.

Tragedy struck the station on December 24, 1935. Veteran keeper Albert Joost and his wife were at the station alone. Joost was using a blowtorch to remove paint when an explosion occurred. His clothing caught fire, and a corner of the building began to burn.

Though badly burned, Joost, with his wife's help, extinguished the flames, and then managed to lower the boat from the balcony. The official report of the accident stated that Joost then set out alone for help at Angel Island, one and one-half miles away. It was nearly dark, and he insisted that his wife stay behind to put the light in operation.

When keeper Spellman arrived from Yerba Buena Island at 6:35 p.m., he found the light operating. The distraught Mrs. Joost was taken to be with her husband. Keeper Joost died on Christmas Day.

In 1939 the bell was replaced by a diaphone. In 1960 the station was automated, and the building was removed. A small light and a fog signal were placed on a platform over some of the original cylinders. Some still lean off the vertical, a reminder of the station's early history.

The building's stately top two stories with the tower and lantern room, were removed and barged to Tinsley Island on the San Joaquin River Delta to become an outstation for San Francisco's Saint Francis Yacht Club. The lens is displayed at an Angel Island museum.

In 1984 the Oakland Harbor Lighthouse was relocated up the Oakland estuary, renovated with care and became L.J. Quinn's Lighthouse restaurant. The hum of the luncheon and dinner crowds provide a contrast to the days when the "BONG" of the station's bell signaled Oakland Harbor to passing mariners.

Directions and Hours: L.J. Quinn's Lighthouse restaurant is located at 51 Embarcadero Cove, Oakland.

TED NELSON

Yerba Buena Island's light shines towards the San Francisco-Oakland Bridge.

Chapter 29

Yerba Buena Island Lighthouse, Depot and Ships

Today, the tunneled traffic of the San Francisco-Oakland Bridge roars beneath the neat lawns and eucalyptus trees of Yerba Buena Island. A short distance away, a Fresnel lens still warns mariners and a Coast Guard buoy tender ties to a dock lined with buoys. The light and dock share a common heritage.

In the 1870s nearly barren Yerba Buena Island was known as Goat Island for the goats that had grazed there for many years. In 1873 the Lighthouse Service moved its depot from Mare Island to the east side of Yerba Buena Island. The depot consisted of a small wharf, a crane, watchman's house, and a large storehouse adjoining the main building.

A year later, Point Conception's fog bell was placed above a low cliff on the island's southeast corner. The bell was used only temporarily, and then as backup. By fall of 1875 the island's Victorian-style lighthouse station was completed.

A steam fog signal and its building stood above the old bell and a small wharf extended into the bay. Nearby stood a two-story, octagonal tower. An ornate railing swept around the lantern room gallery of the white, wooden structure, and the door and windows were elaborately trimmed. From the tower, a fixed, white light was shown from a fourth-order Fresnel lens formerly used at Oregon's Yaquina Head Lighthouse.

The keepers' residence stood above, about eighty yards away. The two-story, wooden building had two gable roofs at right angles to each

121

other. Painted white, its trim repeated the tower's motif. The two keepers and their families had a grand view of San Francisco and the lower bay.

The keepers of the Yerba Buena Island station enjoyed a unique advantage. The depot, only a few hundred yards away, was the main storehouse for coal, lamp oil, wicks, general supplies, food and staples for all of California's lighthouses. To Yerba Buena Island's keepers, the depot was like a corner store. The state's remote and scattered stations, however, received deliveries from the storehouse only every three to four months.

The deliveries were made by lighthouse tender. Along with needed supplies, the tender brought the keeper's mail, pay, and the strict inspectors. When the island's lighthouse and depot were built, the only tender on the entire west coast was the steam sidewheeler *Shubrick*. It had come around Cape Horn in 1858 and since that time had carried construction materials to new stations, serviced existing stations, set buoys, been grounded and salvaged, and protected Washington Territory settlers from hostile Indians.

In January 1880 the new steam screw tender *Manzanita*, built in Baltimore, slowed as it passed the Yerba Buena light in preparation for tying to the depot's wharf. The 152-foot long vessel was designed for speed with a long, low foredeck and holds beneath to carry supplies and materials. A crane was mounted on the foremast. A tall stack stood amidship above the vessel's low superstructure. With the arrival of the *Manzanita* to serve California, the aging *Shubrick* was assigned to Oregon and Washington Territory.

The new tender tied to a large and roomy wharf on which buoys, chains, and anchors were stored. The recently expanded facility included a dwelling for the depot's keeper, a two-story storehouse for oil, and a large coal house with tracks and cars for handling the coal.

As the depot continued to be expanded, the symbiotic relationship between the light station and the depot continued. They shared a common water supply from a spring near the depot. The water system was improved to insure enough water for the fog-signal boilers and protection of the facilities from the fires that periodically swept the island.

In 1886 the new tender *Madrono* arrived to replace the *Manzanita* which was reassigned to the Pacific Northwest. During its first year, The *Madrono* steamed by the lighthouse many times as it left and returned to the depot, covering 9,960 miles and making seventy-three inspections.

The *Manzanita* was the second lighthouse tender to serve the west coast.

In March 1898 another type of ship passed the light station as it approached the depot. It was lightship, No. 70, just built in Portland, Oregon. Within a few days its officers were assigned, the vessel crewed, and supplies loaded aboard. Then California's first lightship took up its station eleven miles off the Golden Gate.

Like other lightships, No. 70 was designed to ride at anchor in all conditions of sea and weather and to act as a floating lighthouse where permanent stations were impractical. The ship had electric lights on its masts and a steam fog signal powered by donkey boilers. Over ninety fathoms of anchor chain, attached to a heavy mushroom shaped anchor, extended from the prow.

In 1905 two new lightships arrived at the depot and were quickly readied for their tasks. No. 83 steamed north to take up station at Blunts Reef, a dangerous shoal off Cape Mendocino. No. 67 became the relief vessel for the then four lightships on the west coast. Annually, each lightship needed about three months off station for maintenance and repairs. The relief ship took over during these periods, changing its light and

123

fog signal characteristics to match those of the assigned station.

In 1909 the tender *Sequoia* arrived to assist the *Madrono*. With it came Lightship No. 92 to serve as California's own lightship relief vessel. The depot was busier than ever with five vessels and thirty-five lighthouse stations to supply and service.

When these new ships arrived, John Kofod was assistant keeper on the island. According to Ralph Shanks in *Guardians of the Golden Gate*, Kofod was assigned to the East Brother light in 1914 and returned to Yerba Buena Island in 1921 as the principal keeper. Walter Fanning, Kofod's grandson, remembered New Years Eves with his grandfather on the island. Near midnight, Kofod would fire up the fog signal and allow Fanning and his sister, Erma, to pull three blasts on the whistle in a New Years salute to each passing ferry boat.

While little has changed at the lighthouse since 1875, the depot has been changed and expanded many times. The buoy tender *Blackhaw* now ties to a concrete dock where the *Shubrick* and a long line of lighthouse tenders used to tie to a wooden wharf. The series of lightships and their relief vessels disappeared from the depot's scene in 1971 when large navigational buoys were stationed at the San Francisco bar and on Blunts Reef.

Today, the keeper's dwelling is the home of a Coast Guard Admiral. The lighthouse tower is flood lighted nightly as an extra aid to mariners, a practice begun in 1958. The light still flashes from the orignal lens. But, the steam fog signal that once signaled a new year to passing ships has been replaced by an electric horn.

Directions and Hours: The depot and lighthouse are not open to the public. The lightship relief vessel, LV 605 is being reconditioned by voluteers for eventual display at Oakland. Call the U.S. Lighthouse Society in San Francisco for the vessel's current status. Phone: (415) 362-7255.

RADFORD FRANKE

San Francisco Lightship LV70 in for repairs at Yerba Buena Island lighthouse depot.

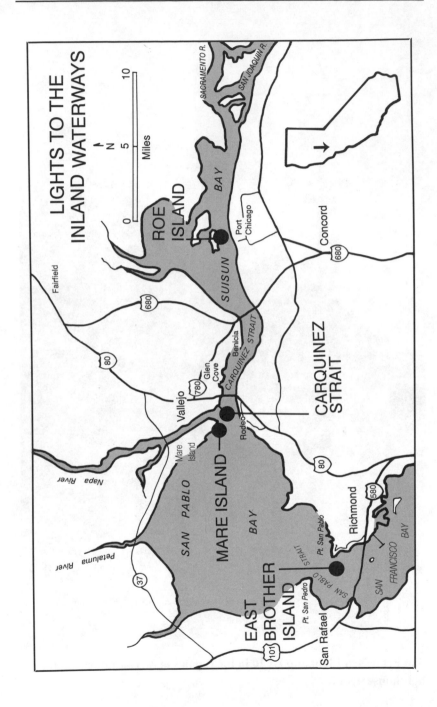

Section 7

Lights to the Inland Waterways

California's two great rivers, the Sacramento and the San Joaquin join in a delta at the east end of Suisun Bay. From this confluence the waters of the Central Valley flow through two bays and two straits before reaching San Francisco Bay.

Suisun Bay (pronounced Soo-soon) is broad and shallow with many marshy islands. At the bay's southwest corner the rivers' breach the Coast Range mountains at the narrow Carquinez Strait.

Near Vallejo and Mare Island, the Carquinez Strait opens into the circular San Pablo Bay. At this bay's southeast corner, near Richmond, the rivers' waters flow through San Pablo Strait and into San Francisco Bay.

The rivers' routes to the bay were the routes followed by the early miners to the gold fields. As the state prospered, the Sacramento and San Joaquin rivers became busy waterways with steamers traveling north to Red Bluff and south below Stockton.

The U.S. Navy's first base for its Pacific Fleet was built on Mare Island in 1854. Benicia, at the east end of Carquinez Strait, was California's capitol for a brief period in the early 1850s. Here, the Pacific Mail Steamship Company operated its shops and a depot, the first major industrial enterprise in the state.

Four lighthouses eventually were built to mark the way to the inland waterways. The East Brother Island Lighthouse is a bed and breakfast inn. The Carquinez Strait Lighthouse, moved from its original location, is the centerpiece of a marina. The ornate Mare Island and Roe Island lighthouses are gone.

TED NELSON

The 1874 East Brother Island Lighthouse is now a bed and breakfast inn.

Chapter 30

East Brother Lighthouse

This 1874 Victorian lighthouse still guides ships, and is also a bed and breakfast inn. Guests relax in rooms reminiscent of its early days while enjoying a unique view of San Francisco Bay.

The light station covers a small island about one-half mile off Point San Pablo at the southern entrance to San Pablo Strait near Richmond. Here modern amenities mix with the old. Like early light keepers, inn keepers and their guests travel to and from the island in the station boat. Wine and fancy selections for gourmet dinners are hauled from the wharf up an incline in a tram car. Water (now filtered) is still collected in a rain catchment basin, and wood stoves heat the lighthouse.

In 1870 the Lighthouse Board decided to establish a light and fog-signal station on Point San Pablo to guide ships transiting the busy inland waterway. The point's land was condemned, but the owners appealed. Rather than delay construction, the Board decided to build on East Brother Island, owned by the army. A lease was granted so long as the island was not needed for fortifications.

Construction began in the summer of 1873, and on March 1, 1874, a flashing, white light was exhibited from a fourth-order Fresnel lens in the forty-eight foot tower. The combination Victorian lighthouse and dwelling was similar to three other California lighthouses built during this period: Point Fermin, Point Hueneme, and Mare Island. The latter two are gone.

Much of the small island was covered by a cement rain catchment basin surrounding an underground cistern. Water was pumped from the cistern into storage tanks. Before rain filled the new cistern, water had to be hauled to the island to provide boiler feed for the twelve-inch steam whistle which was located in the fog-signal building on the island's east end. It first blew on May 1, 1874.

It took forty-five minutes to build up steam to operate the whistle, and fog often moved in quickly. So in 1878 a fog bell was installed. According to Frank Perry in *East Brother, The History of an Island Lighthouse*, a keeper or family member struck the bell until the steam whistle blew.

For many years keepers rowed two and one-half miles to the then closest community, San Quentin, to collect their mail and buy groceries. In 1882 Keeper Captain Charles F. Winsor recorded one such trip. On July 14 assistant Joseph Page left for San Quentin as southwest winds began to blow. Near the island on his return the boat capsized. Winsor hailed a passing steamer which picked up Page and the boat. Winsor, indignant, wrote, "Oars, rudder, mail and all the marketing consisting of mutton, cabbages, peas, etc. etc. lost, also, milk and can."

Winds and storms often buffeted the exposed island and wreaked havoc with the wharf. The first wharf, on the north side of the island near the dwelling, was repaired or rebuilt several times before 1900. One day coal sacks were being unloaded from the tender *Manzanita* when, "...the platform (wharf) gave way and precipitated some ten tons into the water..." The coal was retrieved at low tide.

In 1894 John Stenmark became Keeper, and he and his wife, Breta, and their three-months old daughter, Annie, moved from Año Nuevo to East Brother. While here the Stenmarks had three more children. Stenmark twice rowed to San Quentin to fetch the doctor.

When the children reached school age, a teacher, "...rowed out to the East Brothers Island to teach us," said Annie in a 1967 interview. "But, when they made the road from Point San Pablo to Richmond, we had to row to Point San Pablo and walk the hilly road to Richmond (three miles one way) to go to school there."

By then the Stenmarks launched a boat from a new wharf built near the signal building in 1904, and a mother rowed the children to the point until they were old enough to row themselves. In 1914 when Stenmark retired, John P. Kofod and his wife, Metha, moved from Yerba Buena Island to East Brother Island.

During the Kofod's seven years here, their grandchildren, Walter and Erma Fanning, visited often. "There was a great deal of traffic past the island," Walter Fanning later wrote. "The Monticello line between Vallejo and San Francisco passed each way just about hourly. The *Delta Queen* and *Delta King* made a trip a day."

On fog shrouded days Kofod fired up the signal, and Fanning and his sister joined him. "The signal building was a nice place to be in a fog," he wrote. "It was warm from the two boiler furnaces and smelled pleasantly of steam and hot oil."

The Kofods raised chickens. On windy days they discovered the picket fence surrounding the chicken yard was not only decorative but functional. It kept the chickens from blowing away.

In 1921 the Kofods moved back to Yerba Buena Island, and Kofod retired when he was sixty-nine in 1929.

After the last civilian keepers left in 1945, the station ceased being a family station. Coast Guard keepers rotated on and off the island every forty-eight hours. In 1967 the Coast Guard initiated plans to automate the station and raze the buildings. Local citizens protested.

In 1970 Contra Costa Shoreline Parks Committee succeeded in having the station placed on the National Register of Historic Sites, but had no funds to restore the buildings. Nine years later Tom Butt, a Richmond architect, organized East Brother Light Station, Inc., a non-profit organization. Walter Fanning became a member contributing information from his boyhood days on the island and later restoring the fog signal. The group negotiated a thirty year lease with the Coast Guard, received a $67,000 grant and cash donations, and work began.

Old photographs and original lighthouse plans were studied. Paint chips were analyzed to determine the original colors. One hundred tons of concrete mix were barged to the island to construct a new rain catchment basin. The Coast Guard donated a fourth-order Fresnel lens, and it is on display in the fog-signal building. Volunteers worked hundreds of hours and seven days a week. In nine months East Brother Island Lighthouse was ready for the first guests.

But, work has not ceased. To keep the station in mint condition, each Monday volunteers arrive to paint, oil engines, plant flowers, and mend fences.

131

Large freighters now ply the strait as do sailboats flying spinnakers. On sailboat race days, the inn keeper fires up a diaphone fog horn to greet the sailors as they pass by.

Directions and Hours: For reservations and directions phone: (510) 233-2385. Day trips are also available.

U.S. LIGHTHOUSE SOCIETY

The Mare Island Lighthouse, now gone, was tended by Kate McDougal for over thirty years.

Chapter 31

Mare Island Lighthouse

Mare Island and the town of Vallejo are separated by Mare Island Strait. The Napa River flows through the strait on its way to San Pablo Bay. The island gained its name when a prized mare, belonging to the Mexican General Vallejo, was found there after being lost in the capsizing of a small boat carrying stock to Benicia.

In the early 1870s commercial vessel traffic was increasing on the Napa, Sacramento, and San Joaquin rivers. So too were the number of naval vessels coming to the Pacific Fleet Base on Mare Island. After investigating several possible sites for a lighthouse in the vicinity, preferably on the shore opposite the island, the Lighthouse Service selected a point on the south end of the island for a new lighthouse. A wooden, Victorian-style lighthouse was completed in 1873. The west side of the building had two stories. The east side had one and one-half stories. Each had gable roofs at right angles to each other. Tall chimneys stood above the roofs, and ornate wood trim decorated the building's exterior. From near the building's center rose a three-story tower, home to its lantern and a fourth-order Fresnel lens.

Below the lighthouse, steps and a tramway led down to a graded area where there was a retaining wall and a small wharf. The fog bell and machinery, formerly used at Point Bonita, rested on the graded area, but later were moved to the end of the wharf. The new station made an imposing sight against the hill behind. Eight years after the station's completion, the lighthouse and the life of Kate Coughay McDougal became entwined as the result of a tragedy on the Redwood Coast. The event was recorded by the Point Piños keeper, Allen Luce, in his log dated March 28, 1881. "Our much respected and highly esteemed Insp. Comd. D. J. McDougal U.S. Navy was drowned with two others…while attempting to make a landing through the breakers at Cape Mendocino for the purpose of inspection." McDougal had drowned while going ashore from the tender *Manzanita*. He was wearing a belt filled with gold coin to pay the Cape Mendocino keepers when the boat overturned in the surf. The *Manzanita* returned his body to his bereft widow, Kate, who lived on Mare Island with their four children.

Shortly after Commander McDougal's death, the Mare Island Lighthouse keeper, Mrs. Watson resigned. According to Ralph Shanks in his book, *Guardians of the Golden Gate*, Kate McDougal replaced her, beginning a career that spanned thirty-five years. Kate was lonley at first, Shanks wrote, but she soon gained the rhythm of a lighthouse keeper. She also was close to friends at the naval base. After the invention of the telephone, McDougal's fellow officers arranged for phone lines to be strung to the lighthouse. In 1899 Kate's daughter and grand-daughter joined her, since her son-in-law, a naval officer, was away for extended periods.

Kate's grand-daughter, Mary Gorgas Carlisle, grew up at the station. As recounted by Shanks, Mary remembered the meticulous care that Kate gave the light, the part-time laborer who helped with the heavy chores, and a Chinese-American cook whose work in the kitchen gave Kate time to work in her garden.

In 1910, the Carquinez Strait Lighthouse was built at the mouth of the Napa River, across from the Mare Island light. Seven years later the Inland Waterway's first light was extinguished. The once beautiful lighthouse went unused until it was razed in the 1930s. Kate McDougal lived to be ninety years old.

Chapter 32

Carquinez Strait and Roe Island Lighthouses

The Carquinez Strait Lighthouse still serves mariners, but in a way not envisioned by the Lighthouse Service when the light was established in 1910. Today, the twenty-eight room keepers' dwelling elegantly overlooks a marina near Vallejo. However, nothing remains of the Roe Island Lighthouse. Established in 1891, it was an indirect victim of World War II.

Establishment of the Carquinez Strait Lighthouse was the result of persistence by the Lighthouse Board. The Board's Annual Report to Congress in 1901 stated, "The immense commerce passing between San Francisco and the Sacramento River region passes through Karquinez [a spelling used until 1907] Strait, both coming and going, and it is evident that it is necessary in the interests of commerce and navigation, to establish a light and fog-signal on a point opposite that occupied by the Selby smelting works."

The site recommended was at the northwestern end of the strait, just below the town of Vallejo. The proposed location would better serve vessels entering the strait and those coming down the Napa River, than the Mare Island light to the west.

The Board repeated its request for the new lighthouse in 1902 and 1903. In 1904, the same request was accompanied by the suggestion that unused funds authorized for the never-to-be-built lighthouse near Santa Monica be allocated to the Carquinez light. Still, there was no response from Congress.

Finally, the Board could report that, "The act approved on March 4, 1907, appropriated $50,000 for establishing a light and fog-signal at Carquinez Strait Station."

The first step in building the lighthouse was the construction of a nearly one and one-half mile long pier over the shallows towards the shipping lane. Work began in August 1908. When the pier was completed, a short causeway was built near the pier's end. It led to a rectangular, planked platform built on a network of piling on which the lighthouse stood.

The two and one-half story, wood frame keepers' dwelling faced the strait's northern shore. A large veranda, supported by wood columns, wrapped around three sides of the building. Large dormers extended from the gable roof's north side. The dwelling's twenty-eight rooms gave space for three keepers and their families.

A three story, wooden light tower was attached near the southwest corner of the dwelling. A fog-signal building extended towards the strait. Vallejo City water was piped in.

The station began operation on January 15, 1910. Its fixed, red light shone from a fourth-order Fresnel lens within a lantern room that was dwarfed by the overall size of the structure. The fog signal's air sirens were operated by two gasoline-engine driven compressors. Tenders could tie up at the end of the pier. There was money left over, and a protective dolphin and an incandescent oil vapor lamp were added to the station.

In November 1941 the lighthouse witnessed the end of the era of steam paddlewheel service to the Central Valley. The sternwheelers *Delta King* and *Delta Queen* came down from Sacramento, passing the lighthouse for the last time. It had been nearly a century since the Russian built paddlewheeler *Sitka* had wheezed its way up river.

In 1951 the lighthouse came to the end of its era. The lamp was put out for the last time. A smaller beacon and fog signal were placed at the end of the now extended pier. New Coast Guard quarters were built on the bluff above. The crew maintained a twenty-four watch and tended minor navigation aids in the strait.

In 1955 Robert Hubert, a San Francisco contractor bought the lighthouse, and using a barge mounted crane and ninety-foot long timbers, lifted the 150-ton lighthouse onto a barge and towed it to a nearby cove.

Carquinez Strait Lighthouse at Vallejo's Glen Cove Marina.

For several years the lighthouse languished at the head of the cove, wracked by weather and vandals, and it seemed that Hubert's investment venture was futile. But, as Vallejo grew, investors became interested in the old building and its location. Now at the foot of Glen Cove Drive off Highway 780, it houses a yacht sales show room and the offices of the Glen Cove Marina. The old line of pilings that once led out to the station can still be seen from the town of Rodeo across the strait.

The lighthouse station on Roe Island was authorized by Congress in 1889. Located on Suisun Bay about five miles from Benicia, the island was described by the Lighthouse Board as being, "...not over 4 feet above low water and wholly submerged during high tides." It was on the north side of the main channel leading to the delta and was a hazard to mariners.

The year before, the Lighthouse Service had been given responsibilty for providing lights on the Sacramento and San Joaquin rivers. Minor lights would later serve this task, and the Roe Island Lighthouse became the most inland of any of California's lighthouses.

137

The station went into operation on February 16, 1891. Its fifth-order, fixed, white light "illuminated the whole horizon." The 800 pound fog bell, struck by machinery with one blow every ten seconds, was ready to warn mariners approaching in winter's low lying fogs, called "tule fogs," that butt against the eastside of the Coast Range.

The new lighthouse was an ornate, square, wood frame building, one and one-half stories high with dormers protruding from each roof which overhung verandas below. A lantern stood atop the building's center. A small water tank stood beside. A short T-pier extending beyond the lighthouse's front door held the bell house, an outhouse, and a small building for storing the lamp's fuel. The lighthouse, pier and outbuildings stood ten feet above the island on a maze of pilings and cross bracing. The station was improved and enlarged during its early years. A windmill and pump were placed on the pier to provide fresh well water to the cistern. The lantern room's parapet was sheathed in redwood to prevent leaks. A small levee was built around the island, and the water tank was enclosed by a small, frame building. In 1903 boat ways were added to facilitate handling the keeper's boat.

A second keeper's dwelling and another water tank were added by 1909. The new building was nearly identical to the first except it was topped by a widow's walk instead of a lantern room. The buildings were painted with white exterior walls, red roofs, and grey trim. Perched atop its piling base, the station was an imposing sight to travelers along the inland waterway.

During World War II, lightships and lighthouses of the Coast Guard were at risk from enemy action. Records translated after the war show that nine Japanese submarines were poised to fire on west coast lighthouses on Christmas Eve 1941. The plan was abandoned on December 20th when the Japanese over-estimated the United States' anti-submarine capability.

Ironically, the Roe Island station, the most inland of California's lighthouses, was the only west coast station to be damaged in a war related incident. It was hit by "friendly fire."

During the war, Port Chicago on the south side of Suisun Bay became a major shipping point for ammunition. Train loads of munitions rolled in for loading aboard ships bound to the South Pacific. During the night of July 17, 1944, a train arrived as two vessels were being loaded. Shortly after the train's arrival, Port Chicago blew up, and over three hundred men were killed. The facility, train, the two cargo ships, and two Coast Guard security vessels were lost.

Three thousand yards to the north, the light station suffered serious damage. The bell house was blown toward the lighthouse. The south facing water tank frame was cracked, windows were knocked akimbo, and the widow's walk was damaged.

Though repairable, the damage, coupled with changes in the shipping channels and the development of ship's radar, caused the Coast Guard to discontinue the station in May 1945. The lighthouse was sold and used as a private summer retreat for several years before being destroyed by fire.

NAUTICAL RESEARCH CENTRE

The 1891 Roe Island Lighthouse, damaged in a World War II explosion, is gone.

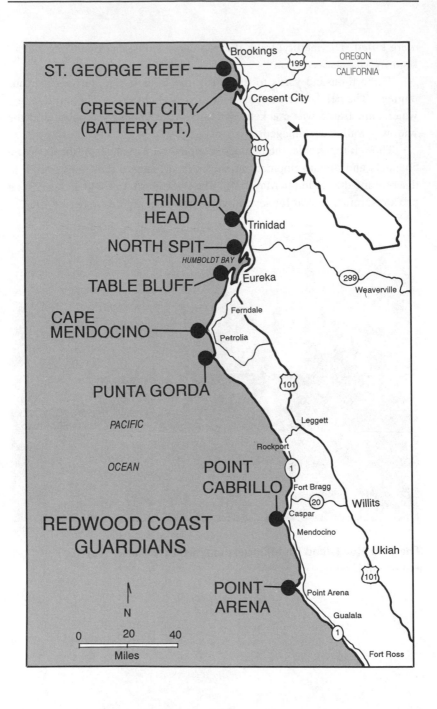

Section 8

Redwood Coast Guardians

A long this coast, in from the headlands and grassy, wave-cut terraces grow the world's tallest trees, little noticed by Cabrillo's men as they sailed here after his death in 1543. Drake came down the coast in 1579, his *Golden Hinde* laden with treasure taken from a Spanish galleon near Cape Mendocino on its way from Manilla to Mexico.

Other Spanish and English mariners followed, but by the early 1800s, the Russians and American sea captains in their employ knew the coast the best. The ships of the Russian-American Fur Company, with Aleut hunters searching for sea otters, probed the coast's unprotected coves and anchored in the partially protected bays. They were the first to cross the treacherous bar at Humboldt Bay. In 1812 the Czarists built Fort Ross with planks of redwood.

With the discovery of gold, miners came by ship on their way to northern interior mines, quickly followed by farmers and lumbermen. Small coves became loading points for redwood lumber. Sail and later steam schooners rolled at anchor in the inlets dubbed "dog holes" receiving their cargos from elaborate chute or cable systems devised to lower the lumber from the cliffs.

Nine lighthouses were built along the Redwood Coast. Crescent City's 1856 lighthouse, Point Cabrillo, Point Arena, and Punta Gorda can be visited. Local museums and other displays provide surrogate visits to the lighthouses abandoned or not accessible including St. George Reef, Trinidad Head, Cape Mendocino, and two stations on Humboldt Bay.

TED NELSON

Point Arena's light station is open for overnight accommodations.

Chapter 33

Point Arena Lighthouse

Point Arena's first lighthouse was one of California's three classic, seacoast towers including Piedras Blancas and Pigeon Point built in the 1870s. Today's tower, its modern look with smooth, reinforced concrete sides rising 115 feet is deceiving. It was built by hand to replace the original tower. The light station still serves as a navigation aid and is open for day visits and overnight stays.

Point Arena is the first prominent point north of Point Reyes, its long, bare plateau with deep, serrated edges rise fifty feet above the water. In the 1800s mariners sailed close to the coast and used land features like Point Arena to help determine their position. When they ran into fogs or storms, they sometimes grounded on the rock-bound shores. During a gale in November 1865, ten ships sank in the waters near Point Arena.

To avert more disasters construction began on the lighthouse in 1869. Bricks were baked in kilns at the site, while 114,000 more were shipped from San Francisco to build the outside courses of the tower.

On May 1, 1870, the first light was exhibited. A first-order Fresnel lens displayed a fixed, white light atop the 100-foot tower that resembled the Pigeon Point Lighthouse. Near the tower's base stood the keepers' dwelling, a two and one half-story brick fourplex. Eighteen months later the fog signal, a twelve-inch steam whistle, began operation.

Earthquake shocks rattled the station in the late 1800s shaking keepers in their beds but causing little or no damage. It was different when the April 1906 earthquake hit. The tower was badly cracked, and part of the dwelling broke apart. The second fog-signal building, built in 1896, survived. It still stands today.

Bids to build a new tower and keepers' dwellings were too high, and the Lighthouse Engineers decided to do the work themselves. In an article in *The Keeper's Log*, Walter White, who worked on the project, recounted the details.

Temporary quarters for the keepers and workmen were built, then White and others began to tear down the old tower. Window frames, stairs, and landings were removed to be used in the new tower. "The lantern and lens had to be carefully marked piece by piece so that it could be placed on a temporary 30 foot tower." This tower exhibited a light in January 1907.

The new tower, constructed of reinforced concrete, was the first of its kind in the nation. "The reinforced iron was threaded by hand, to the top of the tower," wrote White. Cement was mixed by hand. A crude elevator pulled by a mule lifted wheelbarrows of cement. White then poured it into the forms as they rose higher and higher until the tower was finished.

The light from the new tower was shown late in 1908. The characteristic was changed. The rotating, first-order Fresnel lens, floating on a bed of mercury flashed white twice every six seconds. The lens is still in the tower.

Keepers' wives in the 1920s and 1930s found the single-family homes built after the earthquake comfortable. Kitchens were large and airy, and the wood and coal stoves for cooking and heating kept away the chill from fog and wind. One wife learned quickly about the wind when her wash blew away.

Arvel and Helga Settles arrived in 1924. "That was a lovely place to live," said Helga. Their prior station, Point Arguello, was isolated. At Point Arena, "You could drive into town. It wasn't very far, and you could fish."

One day while fishing, Helga, seven months pregnant, fell off an eroding bluff, "...right into the water and went down two times." Arvel heard Helga's screams. He rescued her, and rushed her to the doctor. Shaken and badly scratched, she returned home, then two months later their son Charles was born.

The William Owens and their six daughters began to witness change after they arrived at Point Arena in 1937. Wife, Cora, told their story in *The Keeper's Log*. Owens remained a civilian when the Coast Guard took over, and was head keeper during World War II. Extra coast guardsmen were billeted at the station. Some patrolled beaches on foot or horseback. Windows were blackened. At night cars were driven with parking lights instead of headlights.

Early one morning Owens thought he saw a submarine about a mile from shore. He called Coast Guard authorities, and was told that, "There are no subs in these waters..." The next day a lumber schooner was sunk by a Japanese submarine north of the station.

One morning in September 1949 Owens sat at the breakfast table. A heavy fog shrouded the point, and the fog-signal was blaring. Then he heard iron grinding on rock. The British freighter *Pacific Enterprise* had run aground near the point. The crew remained aboard for a couple days, then abandoned the ship. Waves battered the vessel until it finally broke apart.

The skipper was battered emotionally. He had sailed for forty years without incident, and this was his last voyage before retirement.

In the 1960s the old dwellings were razed and four homes were built for coast guardsmen and their families.In 1976 the fog signal was discontinued, and a lighted horn buoy was installed off the point.

When Point Arena was automated in June 1977, an aero beacon was mounted outside the lantern. The station was closed to the public, until 1982 when the Point Arena Lightouse Keepers, Inc., a non-profit group, received Coast Guard permission to conduct tours. Two years later they signed a twenty-five year lease and hired a curator-superintendent.

With volunteer help the curator renovated and decorated the Coast Guard homes for visitor lodging. The curator's job runs the gamut from lodging and museum manager to assisting television and film crews. Several television commercials have been filmed at the lighthouse.

In the spring of 1992 a Warner Brothers crew arrived to film lighthouse scenes for the movie, "Forever Young," starring Mel Gibson. An ornate shell of a Victorian mansion and a gazebo were built in the field next to the station. World War II B25s buzzed the light tower and landed in the field. After eight days of filming, Gibson and the crews were gone as quickly as they had come. Only the gazebo remains sharing the treeless point with the station's buildings and tall tower.

Directions and Hours: The lighthouse station is open every day from 11 A.M. to 2:30 P.M. Summer weekends and holidays it is open 10 A.M. to 3:30 P.M. Overnight lodging is available, two-nights minimum required. Phone: (707) 882-2777. Turn west off Highway 1 at Rollerville Junction midway between Manchester and the town of Point Arena.

Point Cabrillo's light tower and fog-signal building still stand. The original lens remains in the tower.

146

Chapter 34

Point Cabrillo Lighthouse

Point Cabrillo is a low, sea-terraced point between the towns of Mendocino and Fort Bragg. A small light tower attached to a fog-signal building, built in 1909, and another small building nearby, stand solitarily on the point.

Until 1850 the point's grassy expanse was only a landmark for mariners and home to Pomo Indians. In that year the brig *Frolic*, bound for San Francisco from Hong Kong, went aground off the point and sank in its northern cove.

The Indians were the first salvors at the wreck. Silk, camphor trunks, and lacquerware washed ashore. According to James P. Delgado in *To California By Sea*, Jerome Ford, an associate of Henry Meiggs, a San Francisco lumberman, learned of the wreck. He came to the point in 1851 intent on further salvage, but found such work was impractical. On his return to San Francisco, Ford talked with Meiggs, who was impressed by Ford's account of the vast stands of redwoods along the Mendocino coast.

Meiggs with Ford and two others moved quickly. Sawmill machinery was ordered from the east, and in 1852 the group built a mill at the mouth of Big River, south of the point. Their mill was the forerunner of the literally hundreds of sawmills that shipped their product from the "dog holes" of the Mendocino coast.

In 1905 the Secretary of Commerce and Labor, in a letter to the Senate Commerce Committee said, "...that a lighthouse near Point Cabrillo would be of great assistance to navigation between Point Arena Lighthouse and Cape Mendocino Lighthouse...a distance of 115 miles." The letter pointed out that the smaller vessels engaged in the "...commerce of the small landings along the coast to the northward of San Fransisco...must feel their way as best they can close along inshore." It also said that a light and fog signal on Point Cabrillo would allow vessels to lie off shore and to "hold" the light or fog signal instead of having to enter Mendocino City's harbor in darkness or fog.

Appropriations were granted, and in 1908 the Lighthouse Service asked for construction bids. The prospectus called for, "...a frame fog-signal building and light-tower...a frame one-and one-half story principle keeper's dwelling; two frame one-and one-half story assistant keeper's dwellings...(and outbuildings)...constructed and finished in the most substantial manner."

The station began operation on June 10, 1909. The clapboard fog-signal building, with its attached forty-seven-foot high tower, stood on the low, flat point surrounded on three sides by water. The lantern atop the tower had diagonal astragals, or frames, to hold the lantern's panes in place. An oil house and carpenter-blacksmith shop stood nearby.

The light shone from a third-order Fresnel lens, flashing white every ten seconds. Standing eighty-four feet above the water, it had a visibility of about fourteen miles. The fog signal was a six-inch, compressed-air siren.

The keepers' dwellings were on the second sea-terrace above the point. A road connected the dwellings with the lighthouse. The head keeper's dwelling was the largest with four bedrooms upstairs. Each dwelling had two fireplaces. A barn, water tanks, and outbuildings stood behind.

Little had changed at the station when principal keeper Bill Owens brought his family to the point in 1952. It was Owen's last station after serving at Point Conception, Point Sur, and Point Arena. The Owens' family recalled their Point Cabrillo days in *The Keeper's Log*. Owens' wife, Cora, described the trees that formed a windbreak around the dwellings. There were large yards, lattice fences covered with flowers, and an area for a garden.

Things were not so serene during the winter of 1960. One evening, "The waves got higher...until they went over the top of the fog-signal building," wrote Cora. Her husband lit the light early and all retreated to their houses. After dark, Cora heard a sound like, "...cattle or horses stampeding..." The source of the sound was learned the next day. The sea had entered the fog signal end of the building ripping the fog signal equipment from its foundations.

Diana was the only Owens daughter living at home when the family moved to Point Cabrillo. She fondly remembered her lighthouse days, but there was one disadvantage to living at this station. It was a toll call to the town of Mendocino to talk with her high school chums.

Diana recalled her first date in an automobile. Returning from town she and her date, Joe, drove down to the lighthouse. As Joe was turning the car around, the fog signal bellowed, "...it startled (him) so bad he threw his hands off the wheel and we headed for the cliff." After getting the car under control Joe wondered if the sound was a scheme by Diana's father to discourage future dates. Joe later became Diana's husband.

In a 1963 ceremony beneath the tower, Bill Owens retired as the last civilian light keeper on the west coast. His commendations included the Albert Gallatin award, the highest award made to a federal civilian employee.

Ten years later the station was automated. The fog signal was discontinued, and the Fresnel lens was replaced by two rotating aero beacons. Coast Guard personnel from Fort Bragg continued to occupy the original dwellings which still stand.

Lighthouse histories tend to dwell on shipwrecks, fierce storms, the remote and arduous lives of the keepers and their families. Often overlooked is a life-style that came with lighthouse living that would be the envy of many today. Diana Owens Brown expressed it well in *The Keeper's Log*. She wrote, "...the quiet and solitude I was allowed and the freedom to grow and explore. The main weather I remember was fog and wind, but that is beautiful in itself, those were the times I loved to be outside. We also had days when the ocean was so calm, with...blue skies and sparkling waters."

In 1989 the Coast Guard announced plans to move the lens to a museum in Virgina. Local pressure prevented the move, and the lens remains at the point. Then the California State Coastal Conservancy, with the help of the Trust for Public Lands acquired the property. It will eventually be opened as a state park, and someday a trail will lead down to the north cove where the bones of the brig *Frolic* still lay.

Directions and Hours: The lighthouse is at the west end of Lighthouse Road reached via Point Cabrillo Drive off Highway 1.

Keeper Harrington and his assistant stand on the gallery of the nearly completed Punta Gorda Lighthouse in 1911.

Chapter 35

Punta Gorda Lighthouse

So remote is the Punta Gorda Lighthouse that the Coast Guard officer who closed it in 1951 arrived on horseback carrying a briefcase. Located about eleven miles south of Cape Mendocino, this station stood on a narrow benchland at the foot of bold, rounded hills that rise nine hundred feet. Only the twenty-seven foot high lighthouse, a small concrete building with an empty lantern on top, and the oil house remain.

Conditions near Punta Gorda created problems for mariners. The *Coast Pilot* stated that the wind, sea, and currents here, "...are probably as strong as off any point on the coast." The Lighthouse Board first requested a lighthouse and fog signal at Punta Gorda in 1888, and annually, repeated the request. In the meantime, nine ships ran afoul of Punta Gorda. The *St. Paul* sank in 1905. Its boilers can still be seen at low tide.

Finally, in 1910 construction materials arrived aboard a schooner. The materials were swung ashore on a highline, loaded on horse-drawn sleds, and dragged a half mile south to the lighthouse site. Within a year three spacious, two-story dwellings, a barn, a carpenter and blacksmith shop, oil house, fog-signal building, and unfinished lighthouse stood on the benchland.

Three keepers, F.A. Harrington, principal keeper, and Paschel Hunter, and W.E. Greer, assistants, moved into the dwellings and fired up the fog-signal on June 22, 1911. The light was first exhibited on January 15, 1912, from a fourth-order lens.

Punta Gorda was always difficult to reach. Supplies arrived by boat until 1915. Then a wagon route was cleared to Petrolia eleven miles inland. It followed the beach, crossed creeks, and hugged the Mattole River.

Winter flooding and landslides rendered the route impassable from fall to early spring. When the keepers did travel to Petrolia, they hitched horses to a wagon, hiked, or rode horseback.

Wayne Piland, his wife, young son, and daughter, Nancy, lived at the station from 1934 to 1935. In an unpublished manuscript Nancy recalled one of the horses, Old Bill. Born at a light station, Old Bill served at Point Reyes before coming to Punta Gorda. He, "...was mean and onry," she wrote. But, Piland mastered Old Bill and rode him to fetch the mail. After thirty years with the Lighthouse Service, Old Bill was retired to Ferndale.

Even after the Coast Guard took over in 1939, conditions barely changed. During World War II, a USO representative arrived by horse and buggy. In 1945 the clockwork machinery was still cranked by hand to rotate the lens. Later, five generators were installed, and roads were improved for motorized vehicles.

Still, the station was costly to maintain, and the road continued to wash out. Navigation technology had improved, and the need for the light diminished. In 1951 a lighted whistle buoy was anchored near the outer most rocks, and the station was boarded up.

In 1963 the property was transferred to the Bureau of Land Management. Squatters later moved into the old dwellings, were evicted, and in 1970 the BLM burned the buildings, except the oil house and light tower.

Later the BLM nominated the station to the National Register of Historic Places where it was listed in 1976. With help from members of the California Conservancy Corps, the two remaining structures were restored and painted in 1989. The project took several days, and the crew camped at the station. In the evenings around a campfire, BLM archeologist, Marlene Greenway, shared old photos and stories about the Punta Gorda Lighthouse.

Directions and Hours: From Petrolia turn west onto Lighthouse Road. Park at the end of the road, and follow the trail, about three and a half miles to the lighthouse. Dress warmly, winds can be cold.

Chapter 36

Cape Mendocino Lighthouse

Cape Mendocino is the most western point in California. Seafarers since Spanish explorers in the 1500s used it as a landmark to note their position as they sailed the west coast. The cape's face lashed by winds rises steeply from rocky shores. Near the top it rolls inland in high mounded, grass covered hills, cut by deep ravines. Off shore, rocks, some covered at high tide, and submerged ledges lay scatterd to Blunt's Reef three miles from the cape.

Isolated and far from the nearest town, Cape Mendocino was not an ideal place to live. Still, a light was needed here to guide numerous lumber and steam ships plying the coast in the mid-1800s.

In September 1867 the tender *Shubrick* steaming north with supplies and men to build the lighthouse was wrecked thirty miles south of the cape. The materials were lost, but the tender was salvaged.

A second ship delivered materials a couple months later. They were hauled up the cape's steep slopes by men, mules, and a derrick. Within a year a barn, a two-story brick dwelling, and carpenter shop stood on the lonely cape. Two hundred yards down the hillside a concrete foundation perched 422 feet above the sea was ready for the tower.

Joseph Bein, a machinist, made the tower's sixteen, iron sides in San Francisco, and installed them at the site. Later, he built the same type tower at Point Reyes.

Afraid the lantern and lens might be damaged if landed through the surf, the Lighthouse Service shipped them to Eureka. Here they were loaded on wagons and hauled forty miles.

153

The light was first shown from atop the forty-three foot tower on December 1, 1868. Its revolving white light beamed from a first-order Fresnel lens. And, the Lighthouse Board reported, "...the difficult task is done." Little did they know, this was just the beginning.

Battered by winds, shaken by earthquakes, the new station was a difficult one to tend, and six dwellings were built over the next forty years. During its first decade, an earthquake shook the first dwelling apart and a new one was built. In 1873 an earthquake wrenched the ground open fifteen feet from the tower. The split was filled with concrete. The winds knocked down brick chimneys and broke windows.

Even though there was no fog signal, difficulties tending the light required three keepers. On stormy winter nights keepers plunged from their warm homes into the darkness. Pounded by winds and rains, they found little comfort when they reached the watch room. There was no warming stove. "It is injurious to the health of the keepers to stand watch in their cold, wet clothing," reported the Board. Soon afterward, sleeping quarters with two bunks and a stove were built next to the tower.

In 1876 A.P. Marble, his wife, and children arrived at Cape Mendocino from the Humboldt Bay Lighthouse. While Marble was keeper, supplies and inspectors arrived on the lighthouse tender. Coming by sea, even with the cape's treacherous waters, was the quickest access. In 1881 Inspector D.J. McDougal with a friend and a seaman rowed towards shore. Large breakers capsized the boat and all three men drowned.

Marble served as principal keeper until November 1, 1891, when, "W.C. Price arrived today with his baggage in a 4 horse team to take over the station, was well treated by the old keeper, Mr. Marble."

A year later Price experienced the fury of Cape Mendocino's storms. On December 24, 1892, he wrote in the station log, "Keeper vacating dwellings on account of the great portion of the roof blowing off, blowing the chimneys down... wrenching window shutters off their hinges..." The keepers, their wives and children moved to the tower. On Christmas Day they moved to the stable. The next day, "Gale sprung up again at night blowing a more furious gale..." Price considered moving back to the tower, but was afraid the women and children would be blown off the cape, and they remained in the stable. Winds finally abated, and they moved home.

MARLENE GREENWAY, BUREAU OF LAND MANAGEMENT

Cape Mendocino's tower stands forlornly in fog. Its original first-order lens can be seen in Ferndale.

155

In 1896 the twenty-three year old dwelling was rebuilt. It would not accommodate all the keepers, and one family lived in the oil house, which the Lighthouse Board described as "...almost uninhabitable on account of its bad and unsanitary conditions." The 1906 earthquake damaged the dwelling and oil house, and two years later two large spacious dwellings similar to those at Punta Gorda were built.

Since the late 1890s, a rough road connected the station with a county road. It was improved, and by the time the Coast Guard took over in 1939 keepers drove their cars to their front doors. In 1951 the station was automated, and the Fresnel lens was sent to Ferndale. In the 1960s the wood structures were burned down.

Today a modern optic on a white pole serves as the light. The empty tower still clings precariously to the bluff, its two iron doors pulled off by vandals, while its concrete slabs sustained more damage in the 1992 earthquake.

Directions and Hours: The station is closed to the public. The lens, in a tower replica, can be seen any time at the Humboldt County Fairgrounds in Ferndale.

Chapter 37

Humboldt Bay's Lighthouses

Two lighthouses were built to mark Humboldt Bay. The first, on the bay's North Spit, was completed in 1856. It was replaced in 1892 by a lighthouse on Table Bluff on the south side of the bay's entrance.

Humboldt Bay, California's largest bay north of San Francisco, escaped the notice of early coastal explorers. In 1806 a group of hunters, including Aleut Indians, came to the bay in small boats. They were under the command of Capt. Jonathan Winship, an employee of the Russian-American Fur Company. Winship then brought his ship across the bay's bar, a bar still described by the *Coast Pilot* as, "...dangerous to strangers."

In the 1850s several small towns sprang up along the bay's shores as miners came by ship headed to the Klamath and Trinity rivers' gold districts. The bay's commercial activity, size and location led the Lighthouse Service to include a lighthouse on the bay as one of the first seven to be built in California.

Construction of the bay's first lighthouse was under the contract with Gibbons and Kelly, with supplies and workmen to be brought in by the bark *Oriole*. Before work could begin, the *Oriole* was sunk delivering supplies to build Washington Territory's Cape Disappointment Lighthouse. The loss of the bark, without loss of lives, set construction back. It wasn't until December 20, 1856, that the first Humboldt Bay light shone.

The fixed, white light beamed from a fourth-order Fresnel lens. The lens was mounted in a twenty-one foot high tower rising through the center of a Cape Cod style dwelling. Its range was only about fourteen miles to

TED NELSON

The Table Bluff Lighthouse relocated to Eureka's Woodley Island.

sea and, according to the 1869 *Coast Pilot*, it was subject to being, "...obscured by the mist hanging over the surf on the beach."

In May 1874 a twelve-inch steam whistle was added. More help was then needed at the station, and the wood shed was altered to accommodate one assistant keeper and his family.

At the same time, natural forces began gnawing at the spit. In 1869 the Lighthouse Board confidently reported that, "The foundation of the (lighthouse) appears to be quite secure as sand dunes are forming around it..." However, five years later, keeper George Seeva wrote in the log, "...the bank of sand on the beach west of the lighthouse has been washed away...the sea at high tide approaches the lighthouse about 150 feet nearer than before." Then in 1876, keeper Thomas Winship's log entry stated, "Water came over from the western beach ...Came within 20 feet of lighthouse."

While the sea ate at the spit, earthquakes regularly wracked the structure. An 1877 quake, "...caused cracks in the walls of the tower and the keepers dwelling." Iron stays were added to hold the walls together. Five years later, the south gable was separated from the rest of the building by an earthquake. The gable was, "...temporarily strengthened by two heavy timber braces."

In an 1885 storm, "...the cellar of the old dwelling and tower was filled with water." The building was considered "unsafe for Occupancy" and the Lighthouse Board decided that Table Bluff was a better place for the station's light.

While the Board awaited appropriations for a new lighthouse on Table Bluff, the light in the old tower continued to shine out through the mist. A new dwelling was built to house the keeper on the spit.

Then appropriations for the new light were obtained in early 1891, and construction began in May 1892. The Table Bluff light was first displayed that Halloween.

The fourth-order lens from the old lighthouse was installed at the new station. Its characteristic was changed from fixed to white flashing every five seconds. The light shone from a lantern atop a thirty-five foot tower. The bluff's height put the lantern's focal plane 187 feet above the bay, increasing the light's range to twenty miles.

The tower was attached to a two-story, Victorian keeper's dwelling, built of redwood with the same plans used to construct the lighthouses at

Ballast Point and San Luis Obispo. It was later tied down with cables to secure it against the wind. A duplex for two assistant keepers stood nearby. A windmill pumped water from an ample well to service the dwellings and the two boilers for the fog signal.

Even with the establishment of the new station, the fog signal at the first lighthouse remained in operation. A keeper lived there in one of the newer dwellings. He tended the fog signal and was responsible for tending several harbor lights consisting of "lanterns on poles." They were established when the bay's entrance jetties were completed in the 1890s. A small wharf for holding supplies extended into the bay from the spit.

"Captain Harry" was such a keeper. In the early 1900s he made "...daily trips in his small boat to trim the lights..." recalled Carl M. Christensen in the *Humboldt Historian*. This also meant a stop at the City Slip where he picked up mail and supplies for people living at or near the fog signal and the Life-Saving Station on the spit.

Just as "Captain Harry" had been popular with the residents of the North Spit, the Table Bluff station became popular with many residents of the area. A 1931 newspaper article reported, "Visitors are welcome at Table Bluff and may inspect the lighthouse ...on weekdays." The article noted that weekend visits had been resticted because, "...there was such a rush that keepers were unable to tend to their required duties...."

During World War II, the Table Bluff station was expanded to accommodate mounted beach patrols, a coastal lookout, and a radio compass station. After the war, the keepers' dwelling was razed. The tower was left standing.

In 1953 the station became one of the first to be automated. A smaller lens was installed, and the original lens was sent to San Diego's first Point Loma lighthouse for display. The fog signal was discontinued. In 1975 the station was abandoned, and the property was sold to a private foundation. The still standing 1892 tower began deteriorating until Ray Glavich stepped in.

Glavich and other volunteers, with permission from the foundation, cut the tower in half and trucked it to Eureka. In mint condition, it now stands at the Woodley Island Marina. Other reminders of the bay's lighthouse history can be seen at the Humboldt Bay Maritime Museum, including the bay's original fourth-order lens returned from San Diego and the cupola from the original North Spit tower.

Humboldt Bay's first lighthouse shaken by earthquakes was shorn up by timbers.

Directions and Hours: To reach Woodley Island, take Highway 255 north off 101 and follow the signs. The Maritime Museum is located on 2nd Street behind the Carson Mansion. Hours are 11 A.M. to 4 P.M. Phone (707) 444-9440.

TED NELSON

A replica of Trinidad Head Lighthouse with Trinidad Bay and head in the background.

Chapter 38

Trinidad Head Lighthouse

An 1871 Notice to Mariners announced, "...that a revolving red light, of the 4th order, of the system of Fresnel, will be exhibited for the first time on the evening of December 1, 1871, and on every evening thereafter, from sunset to sunrise from the tower recently erected on the southern slopes of Trinidad Head."

The new lighthouse was perched on the face of the headland that rises northwest of Trinidad Bay. The tower of white, painted brick was only eighteen feet high from its base to the light's focal plane, but the sea rolled against the cliff nearly two hundred feet below. Though the lens was small by coastal standards, its height produced a range of over twenty nautical miles.

The light helped close the unlighted gap between Crescent City and Humboldt Bay. It was too late to assist the ships of the early 1850s that came to Trinidad bringing miners headed for Trinity and Klamath river gold. When the light was first lit, sawmilling had replaced gold fever at Trinidad. Schooners regularly arrived at Trinidad Bay to load lumber from the town's two sawmills.

Jeremiah Kiler was the first keeper, serving there seventeen years. He moved into the freshly painted, white, Victorian residence located about fifty yards from the tower, "... with the usual out-buildings...to the rear of the dwelling."

A fog signal was established at the station in 1898. A second keeper was required to assist in the duties and a second Victorian dwelling was built, attached to the first.

The fog signal was a 4,000-pound bell mounted on a small platform to

163

the east and about seventy feet lower than the tower. The bell house was, "... supported on the front by a trestle standing on the rock, leaving a drop of 35 feet for the weights to operate the machinery." In the fog, the keepers walked down, "...a winding board walk and 48 steps..." to rewind the machinery every two hours.

Fog was not the problem on the evening of December 31, 1913. In a Lighthouse Service Bulletin, keeper F.L. Harrington, after twenty-six years at the light, described a storm that continued for a whole week before that evening. Then the sea, "...seemed to have reached its height when it washed a number of times over Pilot Rock (103 feet high)."

Harrington's observations of that day were recounted by Rachel Carson in her book, *The Sea Around Us*. The book's title was appropriate to Harrington's continued narrative.

"At 4:40 p.m. I was in the tower and had just set the lens in operation and turned to wipe the lantern windows when I observed a sea of unusual height, then about 200 yards distant, approaching. I watched it as it came in. When it struck the bluff the jar was very heavy, and the sea shot up the face of the bluff and over it, until the solid sea seemed to me to be on a level with where I stood in the lantern... The sea itself fell over onto the top of the bluff and struck the tower about on the level with the balcony, making a terrible jar. The whole point between the tower and the bluff was buried in water."

Harrington could not say, "Whether the lens was thrown off by the jar on the bluff or the sea striking the tower..." In either case, he, "...had it leveled and running in half an hour." So far as is known, it was the only time the light failed to be shone at sunset

In 1947 a modern optic replaced the orignal lens and the fog bell was replaced by an air horn. In the late 1960s the original keepers' dwelling was razed and a triplex was built for Coast Guard personnel.

The original lens was acquired by the Trinidad Civic Club and placed in a replica of the tower overlooking the city's waterfront at the foot of Trinity Street. The old bell stands beside.

The automated station is closed to the public, but hiking trails lead to the top of the bluff. The original tower and bell house, now with a newer signal, can be seen from turnouts off Highway 101, south of Trinidad. With a brief stop, one gains an appreciation for the magnitude of the wave that caused keeper Harrington to "relevel the lens."

Chapter 39

Crescent City Lighthouse

The quiet of today's Crescent City belies its boisterous beginnings. The town was laid out in 1853 along the shores of California's northern most bay. By 1854 there were three hundred buildings with new hotels and businesses opening continuously. Crescent City had suddenly become the port of entry for southern Oregon's gold mines and the jumping off point for the shortest trails to Yerka and Grants Pass from the coast.

Against this background, the city fathers proposed to the state legislature that Crescent City become the state's capitol and proposed to Congress that a lighthouse be established on the bay. The latter effort was successful, and Congress appropriated $15,000 for a lighthouse in May 1855.

The site selected for the lighthouse was on a small hill located about two hundred yards off Battery Point. During high tide, the hill is an island. At low tide the hill is connected to the point by an isthmus. The point gained its name from three brass cannons recovered from the ship *America* that burned in the bay in 1855. The cannons were mounted on the point, and for years were fired with great excitement to celebrate the Fourth of July.

Compared to others of the period, work on this lighthouse progressed rapidly. The isthmus was improved so that supplies could be delivered at low tide. A cellar was dug and a cistern laid in. Stone walls, two feet thick, formed the Cape Cod style structure. A forty-five-foot high brick tower rose through the center of the building. The tower was plastered and painted white and the iron lantern top painted red. A fourth-order Fresnel lens, with a range of about fourteen miles, showed a white light varied by flashes at ninety second intervals. The light was first displayed on December 10, 1856.

Crescent City's first keeper was Theophilis Magruder. According to Del Norte County Historical Society records Magruder had come to Oregon with his friend James Marshall. In 1845 they went separate ways, but their lives remained intertwined. It was Marshall's discovery of gold, and the ensuing gold rush, that brought early maritime commerce to Crescent City and with it the need for a lighthouse.

Magruder resigned after three years when the Lighthouse Service wages were reduced. A succession of keepers then preceded the arrival of Captain John Jeffrey. Jeffrey's assignment in 1875 coincided with questions about the continued operation of the light.

The Lighthouse Board report for that year stated, "This station is in a dilapidated condition...the light itself is of little consequence." The Board further stated that it should be discontinued when the St. George Reef light was completed.

On reconsideration, the Board decided the light was needed. The necessary repairs were made, and Jeffrey and his wife, Nellie, stayed on for thirty-nine years. They raised four children at the lighthouse. To reach school the children trudged across the isthmus on low tide and were often allowed to leave school early to make the low tide on their return home.

In 1879 tragedy nearly struck the lighthouse and the Jeffrey family. At that time a wooden lean-to at the rear of the dwelling served as the kitchen. As a storm raged, Jeffrey stoked the fire in the kitchen stove. A wave rolled against the lean-to knocking the chimney from the roof and the stove to the floor. The kitchen was set ablaze. The frantic family began drawing water with the cistern's pump. Another wave followed, poured more water down the chimney, put the fire out, but the kitchen was a loss.

Other storms battered the lighthouse. In 1952 keeper Wayne Piland sensed the coming of an ominous storm. As told by Nadine Tugel, lighthouse curator, Piland, "...noted an erie silence...and a total absence of birds." He nailed down the shutters and prepared for the worst. The storm raged for three days. During its course, "The water would hit the lens." It cracked three glass panes and spewed water into the tower.

But later, Crescent City's greatest waves spared the lighthouse and the lives of curators Peggy and Clarence Coons. Unaware of an earthquake in Alaska, Peggy Coons awoke to an eerie scene around midnignt on March

166

TED NELSON

Crescent City Lighthouse, now called Battery Point and open to visitors, escaped damage from the destructive 1962 tidal wave.

27, 1964. In brilliant moonlight she saw that rocks normally visable had disappeared. Mrs. Coons woke her husband, and together they stood in horror on their small island as five Tsunami waves battered the town.

When the first wave rolled in they watched as, "....buildings crumpled...cars overturned while the water plowed down the streets." Another wave followed, and when the third wave receded, the bay was emptied of water beyond the outer breakwater. The fourth wave was the highest, "...boiling and seething, caught in the rays of the moonlight," as it crashed across the bay's empty floor. The island, "...seemed to be sailing right along with it..." as the wave sped by.

After the fifth wave and in the daylight, the damage was assessed. Eleven people had been killed in Crescent City, and twenty-nine blocks of the town had been demolished. Through it all, the lighthouse beacon "ran smoothly."

Wayne Piland was the last official keeper at the lighthouse. In 1953 the light was automated by the Coast Guard. The fourth-order Fresnel lens was removed, and a small modern optic was installed in its place. That beacon was turned off in 1965 and replaced by a flashing light at the end of the breakwater.

By then dedicated members of the Del Norte County Historical Society with the help of many others had begun to refurbished the old lighthouse. The station was dark until December 10, 1982, when it was reestablished as a private aid to navigation known as Battery Point Lighthouse. A long line of resident curators began to take care of California's ninth-built lighthouse.

Nadine and Jerry Tugel are the present resident curators. They enthusiastically guide small groups of visitors through the lighthouse including the site of the Jeffrey's kitchen, the Wayne Piland Room, and into the tower. Their tours include descriptions of the lighthouse's history, experiences with the lighthouse ghosts, and construction details which Jerry learned as he worked on the old building. One room is a museum filled with photos, histories of several lighthouses, and the last fourth-order Fresnel lens used in the tower.

Directions and Hours: Turn west off Highway 101 on Front Street. Turn left on A Street to the point. Hours are 10 A.M. to 4 P.M., Wednesday through Sunday, April to September, tides permitting. Phone:(707) 464-3089. Also, visit the Del Norte Historical Museum at 6th and H streets.

Chapter 40

St. George Reef Lighthouse

In 1865 the steam sidewheeler *Brother Jonathan* crashed onto St. George Reef, a collection of exposed rocks and covered ledges, northwest of Crescent City off Point St. George. Over 150 lives were lost.

After the sinking, the point and reef were reserved for lighthouse purposes, and the Lighthouse Board began making annual requests for monies to build a lighthouse on the point or its vicinity. The lighthouse was eventually established in 1892 and was one of the most expensive ever built. It was abandoned in 1975.

In 1882 the Board reported progress towards a lighthouse on the reef. A surveyor had landed on Northwest Seal Rock, the reef's outermost point. Some notes and sketches were obtained even though, "The sea began to rise immediately after (landing) so that it was necessary to take him off after a stay of only one hour." Later, a civil engineer, "... succeeded in making a good survey...though in the four weeks of his stay he was able to make but three landings."

Buoyed by the recent completion of Oregon's Tillamook Rock Lighthouse under similar circumstances, and undeterred by the difficulties of obtaining a survey, the Board, "...estimated that it will cost $330,000 to erect and complete the entire structure."

In March 1883 Congress appropriated $100,000 to begin construction. Charles A. Ballantyne, who had supervised the building of the Tillamook Rock light, was placed in charge. He moved quickly, for the construction season on the rock was short.

169

A schooner was towed to the reef from San Francisco and anchored near the work site. The schooner acted as quarters for the workmen and a safe haven when waves washed across the fifty-foot high rock. A cable was extended from the ship to a spar on the rock. Grooved wheels rode the cable, and a cage with room for five to six workmen was suspended below. An engine on the ship's deck winched the workmen's cage up and gravity brought it down.

The workers began blasting the hard but brittle reef to accommodate the tower's foundation pier. On the small rock, the workmen had to, "...hunt holes like crabs to avoid flying fragments when a blast took place." When the superintendent saw seas coming that would wash over the rock, he signaled the workmen. They quickly secured their tools to ring bolts and descended in the cage to the saftey of the ship.

In the first year of construction progress was made in terracing the rock. Granite for the pier and tower was found on the Mad River, and a facility for cutting, staging, and loading the stones was prepared on Humboldt Bay spit.

Work began anew in 1884. The schooner's moorings were reset and a large derrick was built on the rock. Then congressional support failed. Only $30,000 was appropriated and slightly more in 1885. During this period, rock quarrying and stone cutting continued and minimal maintenance was done where work was already accomplished. In 1885 the Lighthouse Board expressed its frustration to Congress. "It would be difficult to point out more clearly than has already been done the uselessness of beginning construction without money enough to push to the uttermost this difficult work." No funds were authorized in the following year, and work was suspended.

In 1887 Congress authorized $120,000 and more in subsequent years. With improved funding, work proceeded in a seasonal pattern. Each spring began with the repair of damage from the the previous winter. Anchors for the workship were reset, and vessels were obtained to carry the cut stones from Humboldt Bay to the rock. Gales and high seas hampered the effort even in the summer.

Quarters for fifty workmen were built on the rock. A chartered steamer ran "night and day" to deliver cut stone. The men worked on Sunday's when stone was on hand.

Slowly, the pier and light tower took shape. the pier's lower course rocks each weighed six tons. The sixty-six foot high pier was designed to

St. George Reef Lighthouse lashed by a winter storm. Its first-order Fresnel lens is on display in Crescent City.

withstand wave forces of four tons per square foot. Zinc templates were used to cut the stones allowing for joints of one-sixteenth of an inch. The pier enclosed an engine room, a coal house, a cistern, and the base of the tower that would rise 146 feet above the sea.

In August 1891 the last stone on the tower was mortared into place. The lens was delivered from Europe a year later and placed into operation on October 20, 1892. It flashed alternately red and white, though later the red panels were removed. It had taken ten years and more than $700,000 for the light finally to shine over the waters where the *Brother Jonathan* lay.

Once built, the station was disliked by keepers. The granite walls were dank, the rock remote, and there were the incessant storms. Five keepers were assigned to the station. Their families lived in Crescent City. Rotations were three months on the rock and two months off. That was if there was no sickness, no resignations, which were frequent, and the weather cooperated.

Keeper George Roux and his assistants, all long time friends, were stranded on the rock for fifty-nine days in 1937. A contemporary writer

171

quoted Roux, "...just to say 'please pass the salt'...became a personal affront. It got so bad that we would try to ignore the presence of each other to avoid scrapes..."

Keeper Roux, at age 62, became an indirect victim of the lighthouse. Returning from shore leave in Crescent City, he was unable to reach the tower in a small boat. After hours of effort, he returned to Crescent City where he died, apparently of exhaustion.

Other lives had been lost at the station. One man was killed during construction of the lighthouse. More died in its operation. In 1893 an assistant keeper was lost in the station's boat and "...no vestige of man or boat (was) discovered." In 1951 three coast guardsmen were lost to a rogue wave while tending the lighthouse.

In 1975 the reef's light was replaced by a Large Navigational Buoy (LNB) located west of the rock. Though abandoned, it was not forgotten. Eight years later under the direction of Wayne Wheeler, civilian assigned to the Twelfth Coast Guard District Aids to Navigation, the lens was removed to the Del Norte County Historical Society Museum.

According to Wheeler in *The Keeper's Log*, the Coast Guard buoy tender *Blackhaw* was anchored near the rock just as the first work schooner had been. Coast guardsmen disassembled the lens. They wrapped the pieces in surplus mattreses and high-lined the bundles down to the tender. When the first load was received, "... a roar went up from the crew ..."

The cumbersome bundles with lens pieces, the brass frames, and pedestal where brought to the museum. Here society trustee, Bob Bolen and his wife, Francis, with some help from others, had constructed a two-story addition to house the lens. Then Bolen, Dave George, and more volunteers worked long hours to polish and reassemble the lens elements and the brass frames. Mounted on its pedestal, the nearly 5,000-pound lens stands almost eighteen feet high. It can be turned with the push of a finger.

Directions and Hours: The St. George Reef Lighthouse with it empty lantern, can be seen from the end of Washington Boulevard beyond the airport. The museum is located in Crescent City at 6th and H streets, west of Highway 101. It is open from May through September on weekdays 10 A.M. to 4 P.M. Phone: (707) 464-3982.

California Lighthouse Summary

Alcatraz Island: Chap 23. Estab. 1854. Nothing remains of the original station. Rebuilt 1909. Tower still in use; modern optic. View on island tours.

Anacapa Island: Chap 11. Estab. 1932. Tower still in use; modern optic. View on island tours.

Angel Island: Chap. 26. Point Knox. Estab. 1889. Original bell at site. Closed. Point Blunt. Estab. 1915. Modern optic. Closed.

Año Nuevo Island: Chap. 17. Estab. 1872. Little remains at original station. View on beach walk.

Ballast Point: Chap. 2. Estab. 1890. Nothing remains of original station. U.S. Submarine Base.

Carquinez Strait: Chap. 32. Estab. 1910. Building moved to Glen Cove Marina.

Cape Mendocino: Chap. 36. Estab. 1868. Tower standing but not used as aid to navigation. Closed.

Cresent City (now Battery Point): Chap. 39. Estab. 1856. Private aid to navigation; modern optic. Open to public.

East Brother Island: Chap. 30. Estab. 1874. Still in use; modern optic. Bed and Breakfast Inn.

Farallon Islands: Chap. 22. Estab. 1855. Tower in use; modern optic. View on tours around islands.

Fort Point: Chap. 24. Estab. 1855. Third tower still standing but not as aid to navigation. View from Fort Point National Historic Site.

Humboldt Bay: Chap. 37. North Spit. Estab. 1856. Nothing remains. Table Bluff. Estab. 1892. Tower in Eureka.

Lime Point: Chap. 25. Estab. 1883. Little remains. Walk to fog signal building.

Los Angeles Harbor: Chap 5: Estab. 1913. Tower still in use; modern optics. View from San Pedro.

Mare Island: Chap. 31. Estab. 1873. Nothing remains.

Mile Rocks: Chap 27. Estab. 1906. Tower in use; modern optic.

Oakland Harbor: Chap 28. Estab. 1890. Second station now a restaurant.

Piedras Blancas: Chap. 15. Estab. 1875. Tower in use; modern optic. Closed. Original lens in Cambria.

Pigeon Point: Chap. 18. Estab. 1872. Tower in use; modern optic. Fresnel Lens in tower; tours. American Youth Hostel.

Point Arena: Chap. 33. Estab. 1870. Second tower in use; modern optic. Fresnel Lens in Tower. Tours and overnight accomodations.

Point Arguello: Chap. 10. Estab. 1901. Little remains at station. Closed.

Point Bonita: Chap. 20. Estab. 1855. Second tower still in use with Fresnel Lens. Tours.

Point Cabrillo: Chap. 34. Estab. 1909. Tower in use; modern optic. Fresnel Lens in tower. Slated to become state park.

Point Conception: Chap. 9. Estab. 1856. Second tower in use with original Fresnel Lens. Closed.

Point Fermin: Chap. 4. Estab. 1874. No longer an aid to navigation. Building remains. Grounds open.

Point Hueneme: Chap. 7. Estab. 1874. Nothing remains of original station. Second tower in use with Fresnel Lens. Closed.

Point Loma I: Chap. 1. Estab. 1855. Fresnel Lens in tower. Open.

Point Loma II: Chap. 3. Estab. 1891. Tower in use; Fresnel Lens. Closed. View from road.

Point Montara: Chap. 19. Estab. 1875. Tower in use; modern optic. Open. American Youth Hostel. Fresnel Lens at San Mateo County Historical Museum.

Point Pinos: Chap. 12. Estab. 1855. Tower in use; Fresnel Lens. Open.

Point Reyes: Chap. 21. Estab. 1870. Modern optic but Fresnel Lens in original tower. Open.

Point Sur: Chap. 13. Estab. 1889. Tower in use, modern optic. Tours. Fresnel Lens at Monterey's Stanton Center.

Point Vicente: Chap. 6. Estab. 1926. Tower in use; Fresnel Lens. Closed. View from park.

Punta Gorda: Chap. 35. Estab. 1911. Tower standing but not used as aid to navigation. Hike to site.

Roe Island: Chap. 14. Estab. 1891. Nothing remains of original station.

San Luis Obispo: Chap. 14. Estab. 1890. Tower in use; modern optic. Closed. Fresnel Lens at San Luis Obispo County Historical Society Museum.

Santa Barbara: Chap. 8. Estab. 1856. Destroyed in earthquake.

Santa Cruz: Chap. 16. Estab. 1869. Nothing remains of original station. Memorial lighthouse near original site. Open.

Southampton Shoal: Chap. 28. Estab. 1905. Moved as a private club on San Joaquin River.

St. George Reef: Chap. 40. Estab. 1892. View tower from north of Cresent City. Fresnel Lens at Del Norte County Historical Society Museum.

Trinidad Head: Chap.38. Estab.1871. Tower in use; modern optic. Closed. Facsimile tower with lens in Trinidad.

Yerba Buena Island: Chap.29. Tower in use; Fresnel Lens. Closed.

Farallon Islands Lighthouse was plagued by construction difficulties.

Index

177

Further Reading

Delgado, James P. *To California By Sea: A Maritime History of the California Gold Rush.* Columbia, S.C.: University of South Carolina Press, 1990.

Dowty, Karen Jones. *The California Channel Islands.* Ventura, Calif.: Seaquit, 1984.

Engel, Norma. *Three Beams of Light.* San Diego, Calif.: Tecolote Publications, 1986.

Fink, Augusta. *Palos Verdes Peninsula: Time and the Terraced Land.* Santa Cruz, Calif.: Western Tanager Press, 1987.

Gibbs, James A. *Lighthouses of the Pacific.* Westchester, Penn.: Shiffer Publishing, Ltd., 1986.

Holland, Francis Ross, Jr. *America's Lighthouses, An Illustrated History.* New York: Dover Publications, Inc., 1972.

Great American Lighthouses. Washington, D.C.: The Preservation Press, 1989.

The Old Point Loma Lighthouse. San Diego, Calif.: Cabrillo Historical Association, 1968.

Le Boeuf, Burney J., and Kaza, Stephanie, eds. *The Natural History of Año Nuevo.* Pacific Grove, Calif.: The Boxwood Press, 1981.

Lockwood, Charles A., and Adamson, Hans Christian. *Tragedy At Honda.* Fresno, Calif.: Valley Publishers, 1960.

Marshall, Don B. *California Shipwrecks.* Seattle, Wash.: Superior Publishing Co., 1978.

Nelson, Sharlene P., and Nelson, Ted W. *Umbrella Guide to Washington Lighthouses.* Seattle, Wash.: Epicenter Press, 1990.

Perry, Frank. *East Brother, History of An Island Light Station.* Point Richmond, Calif.: East Brother Light Station, Inc., 1984.

Lighthouse Point: Reflections on Monterey Bay History. Soquel, Calif.: GHB Publishing, 1982.

The History of Pigeon Point Lighthouse. Soquel, Calif.: GHB Publishing, 1986.

Shanks, Ralph, and Shanks, Lisa Woo, ed. *Guardians of the Golden Gate: Lighthouses and Lifeboat Stations of San Francisco Bay.* Petaluma, Calif.: Costano Books, 1990.

Wheeler, Eugene D., and Kallman, Robert E. *Shipwrecks, Smugglers, and Maritime Mysteries.* Ventura, Calif.: Pathfinder Publishing, 1984.

179

About the Authors

S harlene and Ted Nelson have been studying and writing about regional history for nearly forty years. After graduating from the University of California at Berkeley, they delved into logging history while living in a northern California logging camp where Ted was the resident forester. After moving to Washington in 1964, they contributed to preserving and writing about Washington's forest history.

While living in Coos Bay, Oregon, Sharlene was a correspondent for *The Oregonian*, and in North Carolina the Nelsons published a series of articles on eastern North Carolina history. Their other writings and illustrations have appeared in travel and boating magazines, children's magazines, and scientific journals. Their previous books are *Cruising the Columbia and Snake Rivers* and *Umbrella Guide to Washington Lighthouses*.

The Nelsons' interest in maritime history and lighthouses developed through sailing on California and Pacific Northwest waters. From their home overlooking Puget Sound they sail, ski in the winter, and backpack in the summer.